The Management of Mergers and Acquisitions

The Management of Mergers and Acquisitions

Philippe Very

Professor of Strategic Management
EDHEC Business School

Translated from French by John Cooke
EDHEC Business School

John Wiley & Sons, Ltd

Other Wiley Editorial Offices

John Wiley & Sons Inc., 111 River Street, Hoboken, NJ 07030, USA

Jossey-Bass, 989 Market Street, San Francisco, CA 94103-1741, USA

Wiley-VCH Verlag GmbH, Boschstr. 12, D-69469 Weinheim, Germany

John Wiley & Sons Australia Ltd, 33 Park Road, Milton, Queensland 4064, Australia

John Wiley & Sons (Asia) Pte Ltd, 2 Clementi Loop #02-01, Jin Xing Distripark, Singapore 129809

John Wiley & Sons Canada Ltd, 22 Worcester Road, Etobicoke, Ontario, Canada M9W 1L1

British Library Cataloguing in Publication Data

A catalogue record for this book is available from the British Library

ISBN 0-470-02458-5

Project management by Originator, Gt Yarmouth, Norfolk (typeset in 10/12pt Utopia)
Printed and bound in Great Britain by TJ International Ltd, Padstow, Cornwall
This book is printed on acid-free paper responsibly manufactured from sustainable forestry
in which at least two trees are planted for each one used for paper production.

To Roland Calori, my guide, my friend

Contents

Figures and tables

FIGURES

TABLE

Preface

The original French version of this book entitled *Des Fusions et des Hommes* was published at the end of 2001 by Editions d'Organisation, Paris. The book received two awards:

- The prestigious Manpower Award for best 2002 French book on human resource management.
- The 2002 Award of the EDHEC Foundation for the best book published by an EDHEC faculty.

I owe a debt of gratitude to all my colleagues and friends I worked with in the field of mergers and acquisitions. Among them, I particularly thank Roland Calori (EM Lyon, France), Michael Lubatkin (University of Connecticut, Storrs, USA), David Schweiger (University of South Carolina, Columbia, USA), Stephen Gates (The Conference Board, USA) and Louis Hebert (HEC Montreal, Canada). Working with them was such a wonderful learning experience for me. While I must accept responsibility for the content of this book, I am sure they will find in my writings many fingerprints of their influence. I also extend my gratitude to John Cooke who translated this book from French with rigor and respect for the original style.

Introduction

Have you ever had a dream that you made come true? Just like the ending to a fairy tale, when the handsome prince kisses the princess: they lived happily ever after and had a beautiful baby ... At least that is what you think. Your company is now experiencing a new life thanks to an acquisition. Nevertheless, it is difficult to visualize this new life: it is an almost virtual world in which you had no idea of the stakes involved, whether human, organizational or operational. You now find yourself in the role of a firefighter, putting out fires that flare up in various parts of your new group. The fairy tale has given way to the reality of really hard work. Don't worry: most of your fellow executives who have acquired another company experience the same trials and tribulations and find their managerial role as exhausting as yours.

This book is primarily intended for executives who are also acquirers. Handling an acquisition project consists in managing a complex process that is never the same the second time around. The success of a takeover depends largely on the *quality of the process management.* This book therefore deals with questions of management.

Its intention is to be original. My first desire was to introduce a touch of innovation into the way we pass on knowledge. This explains the novel layout used and the book being complemented by an Internet site (*http:// www.verymerging.com*) that has been designed as a follow-up: this Internet site is a technical support to enable the reader to learn more about how to handle an acquisition. This knowledge can then be shared, integrated and passed on again to the people involved.

Second originality: many researchers studying the acquisition process have used inductive methods to establish their conclusions. From a few case studies they have tried to draw lessons, then have developed some theory and discussed its applicability in other contexts. That is why I have wanted to let readers make their own inductions. The use of the narrative form therefore became essential. Executives tell stories to researchers, executives tell stories to each other; researchers also tell stories to each other. So, why would researchers not tell stories to executives? This book therefore contains seven stories about acquisitions.

Third originality: the stories told by executives tend to enthuse researchers, the more so when these stories are related with enthusiasm. Consequently, I wanted to introduce a touch of emotion, of feeling or of suspense into my stories. Is management supposed to be all serious, austere, sad, or even daunting? In my opinion, too many works on management share these "qualities". This can be seen in most of the "company cases" that are used as teaching aids: these case studies are used to incite students or managers to reflect, and they are usually written in a dry style, sticking only to the facts. They are supposed to be outlining real situations. But reality, even a constructed one, is bound to be different, full of feelings that are not expressed on paper. The solutions chosen are rarely the most rational ones. As research into management by Nicole Giroux (2000) shows, narration can be a means of understanding the world. The stories told in this book are therefore no more real than case studies. My humble ambition is simply to interest the reader, to encourage him to want to know how it all ends as if he was reading a collection of short stories. By reading a story the top manager will probably be more inclined to analyse why and how such and such an outcome came about.

I should point out that the stories related here are the fruit of numerous meetings, interviews and research studies carried out during the last ten years. Each story combines events that marked various acquisitions; these events come from several sources and have been sorted then put together to serve one major pedagogical objective in each tale. No story is therefore linked to any one company in particular. That is why characters and companies have been given fictitious names. Once several events had been put together, I thought up the framework of a story that might interest the reader.

To complement the stories, I have analysed a problem extracted from each one. My analyses are based on research results and try to indicate avenues to be explored in the near future. References are made to academic contributions that I consider important and useful for executives involved in this type of strategic move.

To sum up, this book represents, with its complement on the Internet, an experiment in a new type of support, dedicated to the transfer and accumulation of knowledge in a field of management where a lot still has to be invented. Come and share with me what I have to offer. Let's set off on the journey together, starting with a short poem that sets the tone for the book:

Hey up, management team
Can I have your attention?
Is it your dream
To make an acquisition?

You should be aware
There is much to understand.
The process needs a lot of care
And a helping hand.

So, take the time to read
The stories here related.
Then, your every deed
Stands a good chance of being vindicated.

This book is a tale
Full of emotions and feeling.
You won't fail
To find it appealing.

Every story I relate
Is followed by reflections
That will help you meditate
On the difficulty of integrations.

We often hear
That the process of management
Is very austere
With human feelings absent.

You'll see, this is not right
In the stories related.
They'll give you an insight
Into the human problems created.

I do not pretend
To know all the solutions.
So, I invite you to send
Your opinions and reflections.

There is on the Internet
A site to complement this work
A place where strangers have already met
And exchanged more than a few words.

So, dear management team
Use this book of mine
To help you pursue your dream
Of companies to combine.

Chapter 1

M&A failure as a management problem

1.1. STORY: FLIGHT NA3365 TO MORKOUSK

Per Larsson pushed his cap up slightly with two fingers. This was the third time he had done this, a sure sign of his anxiety. The decision had been taken. The plane was taxiing toward the runway. Per glanced discreetly at his co-pilot, Dietmar Hosch, whose eyes were riveted on the luminous dials and switches. He was checking them again and again. The two men had not spoken to each other for two minutes. The only thing that broke the silence was radio contact with the control tower, which Dietmar dealt with.

The taxiway seemed to stretch for ever. Per Larsson could not even see the other end. He tried to reassure himself. We've made our decision, now let's get on with it. Both men could barely make out the access runway. Theirs was the last flight of the evening and it was leaving two hours late. Svik airport would close after they took off. It was pitch black and, to make matters worse, the weather conditions were appalling: a snowstorm had been battering the whole region for the last three hours. Fierce gusts of wind were buffeting the plane, a fact that could not possibly escape the notice of the passengers. Some of them were bound to be afraid. Per Larsson's thoughts turned to the cabin crew. They would have their work cut out to calm down passengers who were already angered by the delay and worried about the weather conditions.

The two pilots could barely see the runway. But, for once, both flight manuals (i.e., Nordan Air's and V.D. Airways') agreed: visibility was still good enough for the flight not to be cancelled. The decision to take-off was entirely the responsibility of the pilots. And captain and co-pilot had made their choice together, after checking the weather conditions. Half an hour after take-off they would come across more favourable weather that would last until they landed. It was not this local storm that worried Per, but rather the series of incidents that had marked these last hours.

First incidents

Per had already experienced many storms. With 18,000 flying hours under his belt, most of which he had done in Scandinavia and in Canada, Per was used to taking off in these types of conditions. He knew that Dietmar had just as much experience, for he had worked as a captain for many airlines, and wind and snow had not seemed to affect him unduly. Per had also come to realize that both of them applied the same thoroughness to their work and shared the same respect for procedures. All the preflight checks had been carried out to the letter – examining the route and the emergency procedures, calculating the weight of the aircraft and the amount of fuel to be taken on board.

This thoroughness in their work was noticeable, but it was not sufficient to make them forget the arguments that had marked the last 24 hours in the cockpit. The plane continued to move down the taxiway, but relations between both pilots remained tense.

Everything had started when they first met. Dietmar Hosch had greeted Per Larsson very coldly. It was their first flight together, and Per pretended not to notice the frosty reception he had received. He understood the reason later on, after the first leg of the flight. Dietmar had been a captain on the same type of aircraft with V.D. Airlines, and he was now being asked to work as a co-pilot. He had swapped seats. He was now in the right-hand seat, a seat he had not occupied for ten years. This must have been difficult to accept. Per would not have appreciated such a change, even if it were only temporary. In six months' time, Dietmar would again be a captain. "The takeover is to blame for all this," Per thought. Nordan Air had acquired V.D. Airlines two weeks ago. And since then everything had stagnated!

Yet, merging the Scandinavian company and the German one had been announced, with much fanfare, as a brilliant exercise in concentration in the very fragmented sector of air transportation. The press and the stock exchange had welcomed the strategy. Everyone expected the profitability of the new group, which would be financed by Scandinavian capital, to improve. But when the takeover was announced, the German pilots' unions had protested. The German company paid its pilots better than the Scandinavian company. How would this differential be managed? The Scandinavians had opened discussions and had proposed a timetable for negotiations, while maintaining a firm line: in order to improve the new group's performance, they realized they would need to review and harmonize salary policies. Top management had proposed a new system for calculating flying hours and rest periods and had then applied this system to their remuneration policy. This new system relied mainly on calculation methods used by Nordan Air before the takeover. The German unions had reacted strongly. They would not negotiate on this basis. They produced figures based on simulations to show how much they would lose as a result. German co-pilots would be the most affected: their salaries would decrease by 15% if the new rules were applied. Then, other German and Austrian airlines had launched a huge recruitment drive, and about 40 co-pilots from V.D. Airlines had decided straight away to join the competition.

The Scandinavian executives, surprised by the ferocity of the reaction, had had to take urgent measures. First of all, they had decided to review their remuneration policy. In a month's time new proposals would be put forward. In the meantime both companies' systems would continue to coexist. Then, to ensure that air travel would not be disrupted, they had decided to appoint some captains as co-pilots, while negotiations were still going on and while new pilots had not been recruited. Training courses had been organized as a matter of urgency for ex-captains who would once again occupy the right-hand seat in the cockpit. It was mainly a question of specifying each person's role in the team, while emphasizing the predominant role of the captain when it came to taking decisions. In this way, the directors imagined, each person's role would be clear and the flights would run smoothly.

Dietmar Hosch was part of the group that had been selected for temporary downgrading in the hierarchy. Per knew this. He had quickly realized that it was a complex situation for both of them. Dietmar saw this change as a demotion. He had the same number of flying hours as Per Larsson, but, in the end, had to abide by his decisions. Per did not enjoy cohabiting the cockpit like this. And, to cap it all, his co-pilot was better paid than he was! That was why, for 24 hours now, both men had only communicated with each other on essential matters: things relating exclusively to their work. At least there was no language problem, as the language used in the cockpit was English. At each stopover they only mixed with those people they knew from among the stewards and stewardesses, so much so that two groups had formed and led separate lives once they were on the ground.

The climate in the cockpit had deteriorated during the flight to Svik. They had arrived in Svik one hour late. A problem had delayed take-off. While making the usual checks of the aircraft at the last stopover, they had noticed a problem with the APU.[1] They immediately delayed the embarkation of passengers and asked for a mechanic to be sent out. They were

---

[1] APU: auxiliary engine which provides electricity and air conditioning while on the ground.

told that no mechanic would be available for two hours. Both pilots looked at each other. The incident was serious: without a working APU, it was impossible to start the plane's engines. Per sighed, "Well, let's consult the manual to find out what we should do." While taking his manual out of his briefcase, Per said in English: "Okay, we'll check our manuals. But I know the problem won't stop us flying." Dietmar looked surprised. He did not reply, but reached instead for his manual. Each man looked for the official response in his own manual. Per suddenly exclaimed: "Yes, just as I thought!" Dietmar then retorted: "No, you're mistaken!" Shocked, both men looked at each other, then they understood. They did not have the same manual! They had each retained their own company's manual, which gave different responses to the problem of the APU. They agreed to contact the airline's ground staff by radio. The person they spoke to told them that he had no answer to their problem. Moreover, in view of the fact that it was late, it would be impossible to contact the experts who worked at the airline's head office. He also informed the pilots that this type of problem had already occurred the previous week. In that case the pilots had decided themselves what to do. So, they too would just have to make up their own minds. Because of all the upheaval due to the merger, the technical departments had not had time to choose or create one single reference manual, so the members of each company still had their old references and instructions. Per and Dietmar could not believe what they were hearing. For the first time since they had come together, they felt a sense of solidarity in their disarray. However, this did not last long, and differences of opinion, based on their own experiences, soon emerged. Dietmar did not want to leave without the APU being repaired. Per was willing to take off without the APU. Dietmar found it difficult to accept the role of co-pilot. The conversation degenerated. Per had to remind him of each person's role in the cockpit. In the end he decided that they would take off, and, painfully, imposed his decision on his co-pilot. Dietmar accepted without saying a word and radioed for a mobile generator so that they could start the engines. Both men had also discovered that Svik airport did not have a mobile generator at its disposal. Consequently, they would have to keep one engine running during their stopover at Svik.

Tension between the two men was further exacerbated when they received information concerning the number of passengers and the cargo they would be carrying to Svik. All the passenger seats would be filled and a large quantity of cargo would be taken on board. Dietmar calculated the weight. "Captain, we won't be able to fill up with enough fuel here to get to Svik, and then on to Morkousk. Look at the figures. The plane would be overloaded. We'll have to take on more fuel at Svik. And if we leave without an APU, we'll have to refuel in Svik with one engine running!"

Per looked at the figures. It was true. Even taking off with full tanks, they would have to refuel at Svik. "Dietmar, let's see what our manuals say." Each man picked up his documentation.

"Captain, I've found it. My manual says that we can refuel while one engine is running, but there's a very strict procedure to follow."

"Mine also says that it's possible, but there's nothing about any procedure."

The discussion went on. Dietmar was in favour of cancelling the flight to Svik. Per decided to go ahead with the flight, but did make one concession: they would apply the V.D. Airlines procedure when they were at Svik. So, one hour late, flight NA3365 took off for Svik. The pilots did not speak to each other during the flight.

The problems pile up

The two men had been informed that a snowstorm was imminent over the Svik region. The weather forecasters predicted nevertheless that the plane would have time to take off again from Svik before conditions became too appalling. They landed in Svik before the snowstorm arrived. As planned, the pilots kept one engine running. The ground staff had been informed during the flight that this would happen, so they made sure that all the safety instructions applicable when an engine is still running were observed as the passengers disembarked. Once all the passengers were off the plane, both men relaxed for ten minutes. Sitting in the cockpit, Dietmar opened a book while Per strolled up and down the plane to exercise his legs. He even did some stretching exercises. Then both men were back in the cockpit preparing the next leg of the flight.

Outside, the blizzard, which had arrived earlier than expected, was raging. A different kind of storm was raging inside Dietmar Hosch's head and Per knew it. "Thankfully," he said to himself, "the flight from Svik to Morkousk is the final leg of our journey together. Then, our cohabitation in the cockpit will come to an end. He's a good professional, Dietmar, but he's also a pain in the neck! I hope I won't be flying with him again in the months to come." Both men then concentrated on preparing the plane, avoiding any exchanges, and concentrating on their respective tasks. The chief stewardess who came into the cockpit a few moments later could feel the tension and she did not hang around.

A ground staff supervisor came and gave them information about the flight. Eighty per cent of the seats would be occupied and a lot of cargo would be taken on board as the flight before this one had been cancelled. The supervisor also informed them that one passenger had created a scene an hour earlier. He had been waiting for five hours in the airport and was beginning to lose patience. The atmosphere in the waiting room was highly charged. Rather than spending the night at Svik, a lot of travellers wanted a seat on the plane, as there was a large number of connecting flights possible from Morkousk airport. Those who were going to travel on the plane had now been selected. "I hope they'll be calmer once they're on the plane," Per sighed.

Dietmar had calculated the amount of fuel they would take on and he gave this information to Per. The ground crew was informed of how much fuel to put in and of the special procedure to follow. With Per's blessing, Dietmar checked the course of the operations from inside the plane. A team of firemen stood by, watching attentively throughout the manoeuvres. The work was carried out in a serious manner. During refuelling it was strictly forbidden to embark passengers and freight. Once the fuel tanks had been filled the pilots authorized cargo and luggage to be loaded and passengers to be embarked.

Per then received a radio call from the supervisor. There was a mistake in their loading calculations. Ten extra passengers were to be embarked, with their luggage. Per was furious.

"What's all this nonsense? Why did you give me wrong information about our passenger load?"

"It's not our fault, captain, we're caught at the moment between two different operating systems. We're used to the Nordan system, but we don't know the V.D. Airlines' system very well. As this is a code-sharing flight, we have to combine information from both systems in order to work out the load. What's more, V.D. Airlines' sales department usually reorganizes passengers' journeys for them when a flight is cancelled. So, passengers registered with V.D. Airlines complained about the deterioration in service. That's why a few moments ago, the front-office salespeople finally gave in to these ten people and would now like you to embark them."

"What happens on the ground is your problem. I'll be overloaded if I take these ten people, because refuelling was calculated to the last drop using *your* information."

"I'm sorry. If they would only harmonize procedures and make them more specific, then we could offer you a reliable service!"

"I refuse to embark any more people."

"Please, check your calculations. Perhaps you won't be overloaded? If we leave these passengers behind, they'll tear the ground staff to pieces!"

"It's out of the question!"

"Very well, I'll ask the airline's operations manager to contact you as quickly as possible. I can assure you that I'll be reporting this incident."

"So will I."

The cockpit door opened just as Per was cutting off radio contact. "Now what?" he yelled. The chief stewardess jumped. Then she mumbled: "Captain, I'm sorry to bother you. The passengers are getting impatient. They want to know exactly when we'll be taking off. Some of them have connecting flights at Morkousk." The argument about the extra passengers had created further delay.

"OK, Deborah, I'll make an announcement to the passengers in a few moments. They'll have to be patient for at least another ten minutes. I hope the operations manager calls me quickly."

Dietmar then told Per that the weather was getting worse. They were informed that there were already three to four centimetres of snow on the take-off runway. The temperature had fallen to minus eight, the snow was continuing to pile up and gusts of wind were shaking the plane. A layer of frozen snow covered the wings. Now they had to consider the question of de-icing the plane before taking off. Consulting the manuals resulted once again in two different responses: Per's manual strictly forbade de-icing with one engine still running, whereas Dietmar's manual authorized it.

"As there's a doubt, we'll not de-ice . . ."

"But that's dangerous!" cut in Dietmar.

"Let me finish my sentence! We'll only de-ice if the weather conditions make it necessary. Dietmar, give me the weather data and we'll look in our manuals."

As far as the conditions outside were concerned, the manuals agreed on one point: there was no obligation to de-ice on the part of the aircraft manufacturer and both airlines left it up to the crew's judgement. Dietmar resumed the conversation.

"I'll inform ground staff that we may not be leaving," he said.

"Dietmar it's not up to you to decide! I'm in favour of going ahead with the flight without de-icing."

A lively discussion then ensued. Per, because he was the captain, had the last word.

The operations manager called. He was overriding Per's decision. Since the latter did not want to overload his plane, the following solution would be adopted: the ten extra passengers would embark with their luggage and some fuel would be "unloaded". According to his calculations, the partial emptying of the tanks would not noticeably increase the risks for flight NA3365. Per slumped back in his seat. "Why so much aggravation? What have I done to the world to have so much trouble all at once?" Even Dietmar was offended by the operations manager's decision. Per informed the passengers of the situation and announced an extra delay of 15 minutes. There was a long moment of silence in the cockpit. Then the pilots rigorously went through their checklists. Fortunately, nothing else happened to annoy them.

The flight crew again opened the doors of the aircraft and the ten passengers embarked. The extra luggage was loaded into a baggage hold. Once these tasks had been completed, firemen took up position around the aircraft. Then some fuel was taken out of the tanks. Twenty minutes later these operations were finished. The plane was ready to leave.

In the cabin

After leaving the cockpit, Deborah Wells, the chief stewardess, had gone back to her teams. The stewardesses and stewards had their work cut out with overexcited passengers. Some refused to remain seated; others were moaning because the plane had not taken off. It was always the same questions: Why was the right-hand engine running? Why this delay? What are those men doing near the fuel tanks? On top of all that were the usual criticisms.

"Since the merger, service has got worse on board your planes ..."

"Before there were never any delays ..."

"There was more legroom in V.D. Airlines' planes ..."

The cabin crew kept their cool. The prevailing tension brought them closer together. On the ground they only mixed with those from their own company, but here they were now all having to unite and work as a team in the face of these difficulties. Even the organization of their teams had been modified. The stewardesses from V.D. Airlines had planned to look after the front of the aircraft for the flight to Morkousk, with the Nordan Air employees looking after the passengers sitting at the back. This tactic for avoiding each other was founded on a reciprocal animosity, due to the differential in salaries. Deborah, who came from the company that paid less, thought that this behaviour was pathetic. She had tried unsuccessfully in the previous hours to bring her teams together. Fortunately, an opportunity to achieve her aim now presented itself: a recalcitrant passenger had taken to task a stewardess from V.D. Airlines. Deborah decided to exchange her with a steward from the back of the plane. The stewardess and the steward swapped places without hesitation. The passenger calmed down at once when the steward, who had the physique of a bodybuilder, asked him in a firm voice and with a dark look in his eye: "What's the matter, sir?" This change of attitude among the crew pleased Deborah, for she was in favour of the merger between the two companies.

To calm the passengers down, Deborah decided to offer free drinks. She informed the passengers and then helped to serve them. Once the drinks had been given out, she thought over the recent events. Her teams were finally showing more solidarity with each other. On the other hand, what worried her was the tension she could feel in the cockpit. She had never been faced with such a situation. "We have a problem with the APU, but it's not the first time. Usually the pilots remain calm," she thought. "And then this business of the ten extra passengers, it's happened before. I get the feeling that relations between the pilots are tense. Bah! Perhaps I just went into the cockpit at the wrong moment."

A stewardess came and spoke to her discreetly.

"Deborah, have you seen all that frozen snow gathering on the wings?"

Deborah looked out a window. She could see that the blizzard was beginning to cover the plane in a white layer.

"You should report it to the pilots," the stewardess suggested.

"Listen, I've no desire to get it in the neck. The more I go to see them, the frostier the reception I get. I'm sure they've already noticed it and have decided if we need to de-ice or not. In addition, the men working at the fuel tanks must have informed them. Thank you, but we'll let them get on with their work without bothering them any more."

The decision is taken

The pilots inquired one last time about the weather conditions. Dietmar had an air of resignation about him. He had decided not to oppose his captain anymore. Per noticed Dietmar's state of despondency and realized that he would have to do something to try and restore a minimum of team spirit. One final decision remained to be taken, and they were going to take it together. Would conditions allow them to take off? Both men followed procedure and immersed themselves for the umpteenth time in their manuals. These differed as to how to measure visibility. Each man measured and then consulted his reference scales. In the end both companies' recommendations were similar: they were in a zone of visibility where the decision to take off rested on the pilots' shoulders. Per noticed again how badly his co-pilot was demoralized. The latter had completely given up on taking a decision. He was simply carrying out his tasks, and reporting his calculations and observations to his captain. Per decided to take off. Dietmar was immured in his silence. It was 14 minutes past 11 in the evening. The flight would be two hours late leaving Svik. The pilots started the second engine. The control tower gave them permission to move off. The plane shook in the storm. Its headlights had difficulty piercing the snow that was falling ever harder. Per Larsson once again pushed his cap up with two fingers.[2]

---

[2] This story, although fictional, is based on a true fact. To find out what happened after take-off in the real story, log on to the website *http://www.verymerging.com*

1.2. A FAILURE ... BUT NOT A CALCULATED ONE!

The failure rate associated with acquisitions

The story of Flight NA3365 provides food for thought about why mergers and acquisitions fail. However, before looking at the causes it would be interesting to discuss failure in itself.

Studies on the success of acquisitions regularly come up with frightening statistics: more than half of all acquisitions do not create the value hoped for. At the same time mergers continue to be highly prized by companies. Is there a paradox in this?

Not at all. When diversification was all the rage, huge failures were already being announced. Likewise for strategic alliances. And sometimes even for other types of investment (new products, research and development projects ...). Consequently, it is likely that the failure rate for mergers and acquisitions is "normal" in the true sense of the word.

So, while this failure rate is not exceptional, it does nevertheless reflect the difficulties experienced by buyers in achieving the objectives they have set themselves. Today an acquisition is considered to be an investment. The price paid for the target company is based on its perceived value and the potential that exists to create extra value by merging the two companies – in most cases this is the added value created through synergies. This price must be sufficiently low in order to secure a return on the investment after taking into account the costs linked to the transaction itself (financing, intermediaries, ...) and to the planned reorganization. So, the problem is simple: the flow of earnings and costs has to be correctly calculated. It's all to do with the mathematics. And, bad maths will lead to a failure! Look at the merger between the car manufacturers Daimler-Benz and Chrysler. In 1998 it was welcomed when it was announced, but in November 2000 it was criticized, as the value of the new group was less than the value of Daimler-Benz before the merger (*Les Echos*, 15 November 2000, p. 22). Were the figures wrong from the outset? Did financial analysts guarantee these figures in 1998?

Well, no! Failure is rarely the result of technical problems, whether they concern the method used or mistakes in the calculations. Different valuation methods have been tested. Their respective advantages and disadvantages are known. Software programs for simulation exercises are available and are widely used. Specialists in this field are nearly always consulted. Consequently, estimations are often right at the time they are made. So, why do the buyers not manage to create the value?

Let's analyse the answers usually given and show that they hide the true reasons of failure.

Apparent problems usually associated with failure

As we have already stated, failure is the inability to achieve, in size or in time, the objectives of value creation. Failure to do so means that the value of at least one of the companies has been dissipated, or that the additional value hoped for could not be achieved. This lack of results is commonly associated with five types of problems the buyer is likely to encounter: too high a purchase price, the discovery of skeletons in the closet, internal individual reactions, internal collective reactions and external developments. We will only say a few words about these points now, as we will examine them in more detail in later chapters.

Too high a purchase price

We are not talking here of a price that, sometime after the takeover, proves to be too high. This type of analysis a posteriori is rarely appropriate, for conditions in the industry, as well as organization and management methods, usually change, as the Daimler-Chrysler case shows us. By "high price" we mean a sum that is not in the price range that the buyer had considered acceptable when negotiating with the target company. In other words, the buyer does not abide by the conclusions his financial experts have come up with. He buys for a price higher than one based on precise mathematic calculation. In relation to this extra money paid out, Dickie et al. (1987) talk about the "winner's curse", meaning that he who wins the competition eventually ends up the loser as he cannot make a return on his investment.[3] Later on, we will examine the reasons that force someone to pay more than planned.

Skeletons in the closet

In 1997 the buyer of Quo Vadis diaries discovered a number of unpleasant surprises some months after the purchase. Quo Vadis cost prices were too high, computer equipment was obsolete, there was no marketing, the production processes could not cope and most of the foreign subsidiaries were operating at a deficit (*Les Echos*, 18 March 1999, p. 24). Even if the buyer has taken precautions and is able to reduce the price paid, such "skeletons" can upset his plans and force him to radically change the mechanisms through which he hoped to create value. Similarly, some of the synergies that had been envisaged during the analysis of the target

---

[3] These authors have pointed out failure rates are high with buyers who have taken over control of a firm for a price that had gone up by 20% or more compared with the initial bid.

company sometimes prove impossible to exploit once the merger is completed. The added value cannot be created the way they had imagined.

Individual reactions

When the value of a company rests on the skills of a few key people, their departure from the company could put the results of the acquisition seriously at risk. Recent cases of mergers in the field of investment banking have highlighted this problem: the departure of several investment bankers, often accompanied by their teams, may cause a bank to lose a large part of its value, as this is based a lot on the personal contacts and the skill in managing key accounts that its employees have developed. To such an extent that certain banks have wondered about the wisdom of buying out another bank: Would it not be more ingenuous to poach staff that work for the target? It should be pointed out that staff departures can also happen in the acquiring company (Very, 1999). These departures sometimes occur where they are not expected: a division manager resigns, complaining that a big takeover in another division is absorbing all their energies and investments; he believes that his working conditions have seriously deteriorated: he has fewer resources and top management pays him very little attention.

Internal collective reactions

Faced with change, internal resistance of either a political or cultural nature can arise in one of the companies. Here, an opposition force tries to organize itself by rallying support for its alternative plan. These people do not want to change their management practices, which are embedded in their own companies values. Such events can slow down or block the integration process and the exploitation of synergies, or have a negative influence on the productivity of one or other of the companies. Moreover, it is interesting to note that, while the acquiring company tries to anticipate problems likely to arise in the target company, it tends to forget about anticipating problems that the takeover might pose in its own organization. We only see the beam in our neighbour's eye ... The story entitled "Sabotage" (Section 7.1 on p. 137) highlights this point.

External events

External events are of two types; first of all, there are changes in the economic and social environment concerning the industry, the country or group of countries that have repercussions on companies' strategies. A change in legislation or a reduction in purchasing power can thus affect partner companies. Second, a takeover brings about changes, not only internally, but also for the other players associated with the industry. The reaction of competitors who feel threatened, of dissatisfied customers or of suppliers can weaken the competitive position of the new group. Faced with the domination of the market that may result from a merger, some customers prefer to find a new supplier for some of their purchases so as to diversify their sources of supplies. In such a case there is a risk just after the merger that the market share of the new group will be lower than the sum of the market shares of the two companies before the merger. However, initial projections are generally based on adding together each company's current market share. So, creating added value becomes more difficult to achieve. It should also be pointed out that these external events are often noticed belatedly, because employees are more concerned by the implementation of the merger and they tend to ignore signals coming from outside.

These are the five types of apparent problems or events generally put forward as an explanation for the failure of takeovers. Let's go back to our story "Flight NA3365 to Morkousk", which highlights some of these problems.

Flight NA3365 to Morkousk

It was a priori a conjunction of events that made the take-off tricky. First of all, there were things that had nothing to do with the acquisition of V.D. Airlines by Nordan Air: the weather conditions were appalling; the APU, the auxiliary engine, was defective; the flight was late. The pilots, who had a lot of experience, had already confronted these types of incident before. And yet, it proved very difficult for them to take decisions. The takeover therefore contributed to the complications. It had created dissatisfied customers and had induced the competition to launch a recruitment drive. External factors had come into play. Internally, discontent led a large number of V.D. Airlines' pilots to resign in order to profit from outside opportunities; another notable individual reaction was the co-pilot's, who felt he had been downgraded. As a group the employees of both companies avoided mixing with each other; when work made it essential to communicate, as in the cockpit, relations were tense. All the more so as they could not rely on one procedure or on one set of clear instructions to resolve their difficulties. All these problems combined made the situation impossible. The inevitable result of all this was a reduction in productivity and efficiency, both individually and collectively.

If our analysis goes no further than identifying the different categories of problem, we could conclude that failure comes from the inability to anticipate obstacles that might be strewn along the buyer's path. In fact, it would seem logical to recommend that greater effort should be made at anticipating future obstacles; by identifying potential difficulties in advance, the buyer can strive to stop them emerging or identify solutions that he can implement to overcome them. The cost of these solutions will then be integrated into the projection of expected future cash flows and can therefore be included in the calculation of the purchase price.

This line of reasoning is, in my opinion, very simplistic.

The real reasons for failure

As Hitt et al. (2001) stated in conclusion of their book about mergers and acquisitions, there is no simple formula for acquiring efficiently. Associating failure with a lack of anticipation supposes ... that the buyer can anticipate everything. Such an assumption is pure fantasy and reveals a lack of depth in most analyses. It encourages you to work only on the tip of the iceberg. In order to identify the real seeds of failure, we must bear in mind five basic characteristics of takeovers: the size of the stake, the scarcity of information, the structure of the process, the pressures of time and the human side of organizations. Let's examine each of these characteristics in turn.

What's at stake

As a general rule, the takeover bid mobilizes a lot of resources, especially on the financial side. Often more so than afterwards, when the partnership is being consolidated and the business developed. In addition, according to the method of financing used, a takeover can have a real negative effect on the balance of the statement of accounts. This is why such manoeuvres frequently create a sense of high risk. This takeover could be very profitable for us, but it could also lose us a lot of money. The decision to buy is neither trivial nor routine. It is often taken in a climate of strong emotions.

Scarcity of information

The decision to purchase is usually linked to future projections. The financial flows are assessed: What earnings will this merger generate? What will the costs be? These assessments are based on hypotheses drawn up in a situation where information between buyer and seller is asymmetric. In fact, the suitor cannot know everything about his new conquest until he has lived with her. He may be able to gain a precise picture of the formal organization, but he will find it difficult to identify those aspects of the operation that are not codified. Proof of this is the cost of restructuring the company, which is often neglected or under-estimated. Combining two structures, two management systems and teams is bound to cost money. Now, the total cost of the reorganization is complicated to work out, because the way you are going to bring about change depends a lot on informal factors within the target company: the relative balance of power and relationships between the different players, the decision-making process, tacit skills ... That is why, once the target company has been acquired, the new owner frequently discovers "skele-tons in the closet" or, on the contrary, internal opportunities that were not taken into account in the initial estimations. Asymmetry and scarcity of information therefore limit the ability of the buyer to anticipate. The projections are based on hypotheses drawn up by the buyer's own people or consultants. The figures are based partly on facts and partly on percep-tions, judgements, conjectures or intuitions. The buyer is rarely wrong in his calculations; what is more difficult for him is to obtain accurate information and to anticipate events.

Structure of the process

Every acquisition is characterized by two phases: the *phase of hopes* in which the potential buyer imagines, anticipates, calculates and negotiates the purchase and the *phase of achievements* in which he attempts to give shape to his project, aiming to create the expected value. The second phase does not necessarily follow on directly from the first one: they can overlap in part. Readers will notice from certain stories like "the Meletev cocktail" (Section 6.1 on p. 115) that the second phase sometimes begins before the purchase contract is signed.

The two phases are also linked: it is during the phase of hopes that the achievements are planned. In fact, by committing himself to projections, the buyer is also committed to the timescale deemed necessary in order to create value, once the deal has been concluded. So, the second phase is characterized by a deadline fixed during the first phase. In addition, the terms of the contract signed at the end of the first phase will have reper-cussions on the management of the second phase: if, for example, the buyer is committed to retaining the staff from the company that has been taken over, the process of value creation will have to take this constraint into account.

The pressures of time

Time affects the creation of value in several ways. Throughout the process, the value of potential partners is likely to evolve. Right from the outset of the merger project, tensions between buyer and seller or a persistent rumour about the name of a buyer could have strong repercussions on the productivity of employees and the perception of the financial markets. The value of the companies is therefore likely to evolve for the better or for the worse once the first contacts have been made between the future partners. As well as these fluctuations, which are linked to both players, evolutions in the environment must also be considered. New regulations or new technologies can upset the rules of the competitive game, the strategies of the different players and, in the end, the value of the companies. In brief, if the value needs to be known on day d, that will not stop fluctuations in the value from day $d + 1$. Nortel Networks announced in 2001 the imminent loss of 30,000 jobs and they devalued their nonmaterial assets by US\$12.3 billion. This reduction was justified by the collapse in the value of companies like Xros, Qtera and Alteon WebSystems which they had acquired in 2000 when NASDAQ was at its height.

Time also has other ways of influencing events. During the phase of hopes, the teams in charge of studying the merger are often submitted to pressures that come from outside or that they impose on themselves. Jemison and Sitkin (1987) described the negotiation process as a race in which the buyers are urged on to conclude the deal. We must conclude the deal before our competitors do so; we have committed a large number of human and financial resources that will have been used for nothing if we do not buy. These pressures to buy, and to buy quickly, provide us with a plausible explanation for the "winner's curse": they encourage people to pay too high a price rather than give up the bid.

If the integration of the companies does not progress as quickly as planned, the buyer will tend to increase the speed of change – the preferred solution today – or to alter the estimated timescale needed for value creation.

In brief, time is associated with value creation in several ways. First of all, numerous variables can cause the value of the merger to fluctuate between the moment it is assessed and the deadline fixed for creating this value, as certain external factors are beyond the control of the buyer. Second, time exerts pressure on the management teams, before and after the takeover.

The human side of organizations

An acquisition is expected to create value and to provide a return on investment. It is only through the combined efforts of two sets of employees that these objectives will be achieved. However, human reactions to change are often ambivalent and difficult to anticipate. Change brings uncertainty and ambiguity. Confronted with a change of owner, minds teem with questions: What will become of us tomorrow? Employees will be working from that moment under a new management team that has been imposed on them. Psychological and sociological factors become intermingled and influence behaviour. The buyer's first decisions are scrutinized closely, for they give an idea of what the new working environment will be like. Even in the acquiring company, the merger can lead to important changes in behaviour, which may help or hinder the progress of the project. It is already difficult to manage a group of human beings, so how are we to characterize the management of a takeover that brings together two staffs that have different histories, practices and experiences? Many stories in this book will highlight these human reactions and the management difficulties they create. And yet, it is difficult to succeed if we do not rally our people behind the project, convince them, find allies and go forward together along the path that has been mapped out for us.

Five characteristics that combine to create a problem of management

There is a lot at stake in an acquisition. It requires mastery of the purchasing and integration processes in spite of the scarcity of information and the pressures of time, and you have to take account of human reactions. The complexity comes from the fact that the five characteristics are interwoven, and these characteristics create emotions, reactions, uncertainties, ambiguities, constraints and pressures. For example, internal reactions are all the more difficult to anticipate when you do not know one of the groups, the people who make up this group, their history, their way of working. Like every major change, when you take control, you create uncertainties and ambiguities in your old and new employees. In addition, you yourself have the feeling that you are running a disproportionate risk compared with the usual ones you take in your everyday decisions. You question yourself regularly about the wisdom of the operation. Behaviour evolves continually during the first months: it changes with the slightest modification to the environment, with the slightest thing you do (or do not do), and this change may favour or hinder the value creation project. In brief, the characteristics associated with a merger project, once they combine, may make your task difficult.

Let's go back to our story "Flight NA3365 to Morkousk". The conditions necessary for the operation to run smoothly are not in place. Certain differences (e.g., in the remuneration policies, or the differences between flight manuals) were not identified beforehand or taken into account when the integration took place, thus endangering the value creation project. But would it have been easy to anticipate these problems? For example, would it have been possible to foresee the reaction of the competition? Confronted with the individual and collective reactions

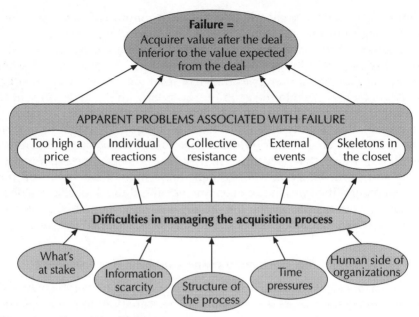

Figure 1.1   The seeds of failure.

of the employees, particularly the co-pilot's, Nordan Air's top management had to take corrective measures and review their integration project. Pushed by time, their priority was to find a way to retain the value of both companies. However, their decisions and actions created new reactions, like the dissatisfaction of the downgraded co-pilot. The human side of the organization therefore interferes with the pressures of time and the difficulties in anticipating events. In fact, the real seeds of failure are to be found in the various challenges created by the integration process: managing a situation where information is asymmetric, driving the process in an appropriate manner, controlling the stress linked to the stakes, dealing with the pressures of time and managing a group of human beings. In addition, it is even more difficult to manage the interweaving of these dimensions.[4] When all is said and done, it becomes obvious that the five classical justifications of failure generally invoked by acquirers stem from their own difficulties in managing a specific and complex process. Figure 1.1 sums up what we have said.

This analysis leads us to make recommendations that are different

---

[4] We do not mean that all buyers systematically encounter the same problems. On the contrary, the difficulties vary according to the context of the acquisition, as we will see in Chapter 4.

from traditional conclusions. Even if a commendable effort is made to anticipate events, this will not resolve all the difficulties. Obstacles do not arise from a lack of anticipation, but from the difficulty of managing this type of strategic manoeuvre. It is a management problem. Efficient management of the acquisition process would combine the ability to anticipate events with an ability to react to what cannot or has not been planned. Efficient management of the process would integrate the pressures of time, the scarcity of information, the importance of the stakes and the human side of the organizations. In the absence of such management, the large amount of work that has to be done, the individual and collective efforts put in, the financial investments committed during the phase of hope, all of these force the buyer to pay a higher price than estimated or to accept unfavourable conditions of purchase. Emotional factors come into play. Irrational elements guide the negotiations on the price instead of "reasonable" valuations. Deficiencies in the conduct of the process may also contribute to neglecting the preparation of the phase of achievements or to forgetting to construct the foundations of this phase in time. In brief, it is essential to ensure continuity in the management of a process that is apparently discontinuous, by monitoring emotions, pressures, uncertainties and discoveries.

Summary

No, failure has nothing to do with the maths! And this paradox calls to mind the classic management dilemma: we have to foresee and implement without knowing all the facts and in a framework of dynamic evolution. Nevertheless, the solution to this paradox is not as classical, because it has its origins in characteristics that are specific to acquisitions. These manoeuvres create more emotions than usual, more uncertainties and more unexpected reactions. This additional intensity and variability in perceptions and behaviour, whether individual or collective, requires an appropriate approach to management.

In the end, faced with the complex nature of the managerial task, it is "no wonder" that more than one out of two mergers fail.

Chapter 2

Ego and geo: Two motivations for acquiring

2.1. STORY: TO CONQUER THE WORLD

"Mancini, just wait and see, Gerd Strunz will put his castle on D4 sometime in the next few months."

Guido Valli, CEO of the A.M.I. empire, surprised Mancini, his right-hand man, with this prediction. How could Guido foresee the moves that his opponent would make? These last few years, Guido had predicted a number of manoeuvres his main rival, the German conglomerate Vanstav, would make. He had rarely been wrong.

"A castle," Mancini thought. In the past the predicted moves usually concerned pawns, sometimes a knight or a bishop. But this time Guido was talking about a castle. This must be a large-scale manoeuvre. Furthermore, he was talking about a castle in Western Europe, on the historic battlefield of these two giants of the electronics industry! Square D4 did indeed correspond to that region of the world on his boss's chessboard. This chessboard was the only one of its kind, made to order: in the background there was a map of the world over which the squares had been designed. The chessmen were positioned all over the chessboard, at different points of the globe. They represented Vanstav's and A.M.I.'s respective positions.

Mancini remembered an incident when he was recruited by A.M.I. Going over to the chessboard he had asked which pawns represented A.M.I. His question had received a scathing response: "You disappoint me. First of all, we talk about chessmen, not pawns. Then we are white, of course. White starts the game and is always one move ahead."

"Why a castle in Europe?" Mancini asked, knowing that his egocentric boss would be flattered by the question. Guido Valli was indeed only too pleased to explain."You know, Mancini, I spend a lot of time at my chess-board. I study the position of each chessman and I assess the balance of power. My goal is not to 'checkmate' my opponent. Instead, it is to keep Vanstav in good shape, to enable them to endure, but on one condition: that we are always the leader and that they stay in second place in the world market. Competition with Vanstav is good for A.M.I. In fact, we have nothing to fear from their senior management; the people who are in charge of Vanstav are not capable, in my opinion, of overtaking us on a long-term basis. But the presence of this powerful rival protects us from the emergence of new competitors. Our two companies control most of the big markets and determine the rules of the game. In brief, we need them."

"Excuse me, Mister Valli, but you haven't really answered my question ..."

"First of all, you need to take on board what I've just told you," G. Valli cut in, "if you want to understand my line of reasoning. Our war with Vanstav intensified after the fall of the Berlin wall. At that moment their nationality became their main advantage. Vanstav began to acquire every-thing that was of value in the ex-East Germany and in the neighbouring countries, thus posing a threat to our world supremacy. Fortunately, we reacted quickly! Our acquisitions in Hungary and the Czech Republic allowed us to regain the initiative: not only did we acquire companies they were targeting, but these acquisitions also enabled us to consolidate our lead over Vanstav. You know, Mancini, the opening up of the East marked a turning point in our strategy, for it was the start of our fascinat-ing battle with Vanstav to establish world leadership. Look at what we did after that: in 1995 we acquired the Brazilian company, Ectro, followed by the Argentine company, Tratel, and we now dominate the South American market. Vanstav reacted by acquiring that same year the Mexican company, Callon, which could have seriously hindered our development in North America. But, straight away, we bought the American distributor US Elt to block Vanstav's access to this market. Remember, we had started negotiations more than a year beforehand."

"That's right. I remember: at that time you predicted an offensive from Vanstav into that area of the world and you wanted to get in ahead of them ..."

"On that move we didn't manage to finalize an agreement before them. But we lived to fight another day. We had barely finished negotiat-ing with US Elt when we acquired five Asian manufacturers in succession and launched our joint venture in Shanghai. You know, that offensive was planned. The battle with Vanstav was at that time focused on the American continent. It was obvious that it would then move to other parts of the world, and South-East Asia seemed to be the logical place.

This was how I saw things at that time: the Asian crisis had weakened a number of local competitors. We could do good business by acquiring the most successful ones. Of course, some countries were in economic crisis and it was difficult to predict when they would recover. However, it was obvious to me that they would recover assisted, if necessary, by Western countries, which need Asia. In other words, I have always believed that every crisis eventually comes to an end; it's only a question of time. Now, as A.M.I. has solid financial foundations, we could afford to buy without expecting an immediate return on investment. And that's what we did."

"But Vanstav also acquired ..."

"You're right, Mancini. But we cut the ground from under their feet. We even competed for certain companies in Indonesia and in India, and each time we were the winners. In fact, today, we are the leader in 4 of the 5 most important countries in South-East Asia. In that part of the world we are also ahead of Vanstav."

Guido Valli's face creased into a contented smile. With the tip of his fingers he slowly caressed the part of the chessboard that represented Asia. Suddenly, his smile disappeared and he began to frown as his fingers moved quickly to square D4.

"Mancini, the heart of the battle moved from Eastern Europe to Asia, passing through the American continent on the way: it's now time to come back home. We have completed a round of relatively easy acquisitions, since each competitor grabbed companies that were up for sale around the world. Today, opportunities have become rare; we will now have to convince owners to let us buy their company. This is a new and more complex step for Vanstav, as it is for us. It would therefore be logical to test this new process in countries that we are familiar with. Furthermore, the battle has diverted our attention from Europe so much that it's time to come back to those markets that made us prosperous and enabled us to develop. That's why Western Europe is about to become the object of our future desires."

"You're right, it's logical," Mancini acknowledged. "But why a castle rather than a pawn on D4?"

"The race to be number one, Mancini! What would be the point of an acquisition worth a few hundred million dollars, and which would only give the buyer a slight gain in market share? No, Vanstav is going to go for the big one. I know Gerd Strunz well. He doesn't like us and desperately wants to overtake us. As his group is soundly managed, he'll be able to convince his main shareholders, American investment funds. They'll give him carte blanche to carry out a major operation where there is strong hope of huge gains, if he can finance it intelligently. Gerd dreams of an acquisition that would upset the established positions. He will therefore be looking to carry off a master stroke. However, we are going to seek to increase our lead over Vanstav. And in this battle, do you know what our advantage is?"

Mancini waited for his boss to reply.

"Our advantage is that we try to imagine and anticipate the moves that our opponent might make. Whereas Gerd and his advisers never worry about the strategic moves we might make."

Guido Valli stopped talking and gazed at his fingers that were still touching square D4. He received the compliment he expected, but it was then followed by a question that irritated the CEO.

"Good thinking: I can see that your management technique is based on this kind of reasoning," Mancini said. "Nevertheless, since each person tries in turn to trump his opponent, where will this competition take us all?"

"Trump, Mancini, trump? For three-quarters of an hour now I've been talking to you about the complex, noble game of chess and you sum it all up as if it were a common game of cards!"

Mancini turned crimson.

Confidential meeting in Vanstav

Gerd Strunz was admiring the sunset through his office window. Standing with his hands behind his back, he was speaking in a quiet voice. The two people he was speaking to remained seated at the worktable.

"We continue as planned with the two negotiations already under way. In Italy go slowly. Olaf, I'm relying on you to drag it out. All the uncertainties or weak points that came to light during the diagnosis have to be discussed. Propose as many clauses in the contract as you wish, but don't discourage the Mossi management. I certainly don't want them to stop the process. It is vital for Vanstav that we keep these discussions going while the American operation hasn't been concluded."

"I understand, Gerd," replied Olaf Spack, the financial director. "I'll do all I can to keep the negotiations going slowly. We do have one difficulty: other competitors are interested in Mossi. If one of them makes an enticing proposition, there is the risk that Mossi might jump at it and drop us."

Gerd Strunz came and sat down near the two men.

"I know, Olaf. We don't hold all the cards, but do your best anyway. Put some pressure on the 15 people in the team in charge of the operation. It'll be essential if we want to achieve our objective."

"That won't be a problem. Each member of the team has a well-defined task and no one has questioned the size of the team."

"Good work. Now what's the position with the Delta Hawk bid?"

Olaf gave him the latest news from their American team.

"Our guys are confident. Negotiations are going well in spite of the fact that the seller always has a large number of lawyers present. We think that the Delta Hawk management is really interested in a friendly merger with us. As you predicted, their CEO is attracted by our propositions. In addition to the very generous financial compensation he will receive from us, he'll also join our board of directors if the deal goes through. And, if our estimations are correct, the deal should be closed in two weeks' time for a price that is not far off our initial offer."

"Great! Let's pray that everything goes the way we imagined. Olaf, I'm asking a lot of you at this crucial period for our company. I'd like to thank you for the excellent work you're doing."

"Thank you. I'm flying to the USA in two days' time. I'll update you daily from Phoenix on how the negotiations are going."

"I hope you didn't order your ticket through our normal channels."

"Don't worry, Peter dealt with it himself."

Peter Guff was the third man present at the meeting. He was in charge of Vanstav's information systems. He had joined the company at the same time as Gerd and both of them had risen up the hierarchy to become top executives. Peter, a fairly discreet person, put his little round glasses back on. Then he spoke.

"From now on we'll have to be even more careful. When one of you has to go to Delta Hawk's head office in the USA, you'll have to order a ticket for another of our subsidiaries in the world. Your personal assistants will go through the normal channels and order the ticket from our travel agency. At the same time I'll buy the ticket for the USA, paying for it from my own budget and I'll pass it on to you. During each trip I'll divert your direct phone lines. In this way, you can be contacted in Phoenix by your assistant, but she'll think she's phoning the Jakarta or Buenos Aires subsidiaries."

"You're right, Peter. We've got to be careful. It's a good initiative. Have you made any progress with our other problem?"

"The phone-taps have produced nothing. The guy's careful. I've started checking their emails. For the moment I've eliminated 12 people from the board of directors. That leaves 4 and, in two or three days' time, I should be able to tell you if we have a result."

"Fine, Peter, keep going. Time is short, so devote every minute you have to the job. Let's set a new trap! Try giving the Italian team a piece of information that'll make them react."

The three men got up. Gerd Strunz shook their hands warmly and said to them: "Dear friends, you're the only people I've taken into my confidence. It's up to us three to lance the boil. Once again, don't speak to anyone about what we're doing. Absolute secrecy is essential."

Peter and Olaf left. Gerd closed the door, slumped into his armchair and lit his pipe. "Let's hope it works," he thought.

A.M.I. in the starting blocks

A.M.I.'s top management was bubbling with excitement. Guido Valli had launched an offensive on Mossi. A.M.I. was not the only one in the race and had arrived on the scene after the other bidders. Guido Valli had had to pile pressure on the Mossi management in order to be able to take part in the bidding. He had won by playing on feelings. Fierce enemies in their own national territory, the top executives of both companies did not really like each other. A.M.I. had had to brandish the national flag and argue that it wanted to protect Italian industry in order to convince its rivals. Pressure exerted by some Mossi shareholders had also influenced their decision. Guido Valli had beforehand devoted a lot of energy to convincing these shareholders of the wisdom of the operation.

Today, A.M.I. was finally part of the group of potential buyers. Guido Valli had entrusted the dossier to Mancini, his second-in-command. Mancini had organized his team and had entrusted several tasks to external consultants. The first investigations came up with positive information. Mossi was well established in Italy, Spain and France, and to a lesser extent in Switzerland and Germany. Its factories were successful, both in controlling costs and in maintaining the quality of their product lines. The main concern was the customers: Mossi was starting to lose big international customers who preferred to centralize their purchasing for all their subsidiaries worldwide. Now Mossi did not have a presence abroad that could ensure this type of service. It was an excellent company as far as local customers were concerned. But, the family shareholders did not want to increase their capital investment in the company. They knew that Mossi could not survive without growth, because both research and development and production needed massive investment. And only a strong international presence that would enable them to sell large quantities of one product could ensure a return on this type of investment. Faced with this situation, the family preferred to pull out and give up their shares in the company.

For Mancini, Mossi appeared to be a big catch. Some of its know-how would be very useful to A.M.I. Their customers complemented each other. If the deal went through, A.M.I. would gain an extra 5% of the European market. Such a progression would be spectacular and difficult for their competitor, Vanstav, to make up. Furthermore, A.M.I. would be encroaching on their rival's German territory!

Mancini thought about what his boss had said, "... we'll get in ahead of Vanstav ... let's find a big target in Europe ... and why not in Italy? ..."

And then Guido Valli had informed him of the secret negotiations with the Mossi directors, before entrusting him with the dossier. Guido certainly had a unique nose for business.

Yet Mancini was worried. Despite the large number of acquisitions he had been in charge of, this one was particular. The target was a huge and successful Italian company. He had to succeed. Failure would mean that another buyer would take control of Mossi. Mancini's problem was that he did not know who the other bidders were. He could only imagine the possibilities.

It was reasonable to assume that Mossi might represent an opportunity to diversify for one of the giants of the electricity or electronics industries. This was conceivable. However, when synergies were taken into account, A.M.I. should be able to offer a better price than those players from another sector. Mossi might also interest one of the five other companies who shared most of the industrial electronics market with A.M.I. If one of the four smaller companies acquired or merged with Mossi, it would have no effect on A.M.I. On the other hand, if it were the fifth company, Vanstav, that won, that would be a different matter. A.M.I would have to share leadership of the European market. So, Vanstav could catch up with A.M.I. in Europe by taking over this Italian target. What is more, they would be on an equal footing with A.M.I. on Italian soil!

"If necessary, we'll pay a high price to stop this target getting away from us," Mancini thought. With his eyes riveted to the ceiling, he prayed that Vanstav was not one of the bidders.

Vanstav's ambitions

Gerd Strunz was gazing at the oval worktable that stood in his office. With both hands resting on the glass top, he was looking at the different regions of the world. Under the glass top a big liquid crystal screen had been installed and a political map of the world, country by country, had been superimposed onto this screen. A blue-tinted, filtered light, directed at the glass top, softened the contrasts and enabled you to look at the map for several minutes without tiring your eyes. Small factories, small shops and small microprocessors were positioned all over the map. These symbols represented production facilities, sales outlets and research and development centres. They were spread out over different countries and represented Vanstav's presence in these places. Whenever a subsidiary was created, the image was altered by computer, and an up-to-date version was projected on to the screen to replace the old one. Gerd Strunz was proud of this table, the only one of its kind, and which he had designed. He pressed a button located below the glass top. The same symbolic system appeared in various parts of the map, with only one difference: the first symbols were all white, whereas these new ones were black. The black ones represented A.M.I. subsidiaries. One fact clearly stood out from this simultaneous vision of both companies' presence in the world: rare were those countries where one of them was present and the other not.

The rivalry with A.M.I. had been like a thorn in Gerd Strunz's side ever since the Eastern European manoeuvres. His competitor restricted his access to South America: he immediately counterattacked in Central America. And the skirmishing had gone on in different parts of the world. An eye for an eye, a tooth for a tooth! What had irritated Gerd for some years now was that A.M.I. was often one step ahead. They had often fought over the same targets and A.M.I. had been victorious most of the time. Thanks to these victories, A.M.I. had left Vanstav trailing behind and now dominated the world market. However, A.M.I. had acquired some of their targets for a price that seemed excessive to Gerd Strunz. Sometimes he had preferred to pull out of the contest rather than get involved in a bidding war.

Gerd believed that the war was not over, even if the outcome of the first battles had frequently not been in his favour. The gap could still be closed. For a start, the excellent results they had returned in these last three years had provided him with extra cash to pursue his expansion. Vanstav was highly quoted on the stock exchange and its shares commanded a high price. Furthermore, Gerd Strunz had persuaded his shareholders to increase the capital. They had all agreed to finance future international operations if necessary. The breakdown of the shareholders between investment funds, banks and the general public would not be altered by the next cross-border operations, and Gerd was pleased about this. When he had called a meeting of his board to outline his plans to purchase simultaneously in Italy and the USA, he had been given the go-ahead. Convincing them had been easy and he was greatly indebted to his Strategy Department for this. Company strategists had studied the political and economic risks associated with a large number of countries, had analysed their potential for growth, had identified the internationalization strategies of their big customers and their main competitors, and had weighed up the economic downturns that might affect Vanstav in the future. Their investigations were written up in a thick dossier that concluded that it was in Vanstav's interest to invest in the developed world. Their arguments proved conclusive and the choice of Italy and the USA was easily ratified.

The acquisition process swung into operation in each continent. Acquiring Delta Hawk was the priority. Gerd was determined to close this deal for it would make his company the leader in North America.

The competition was fragmented on this continent. No competitor held more than 18% of the market. In acquiring Delta Hawk, the biggest American manufacturer of industrial electronics, Vanstav would corner 30% of local sales and would quite obviously dominate the competition. The advantage could be decisive: after the takeover, Vanstav would make substantial savings on components purchasing and would benefit from large economies of scale in production. Moreover, according to the external experts commissioned to study Delta Hawk, one of Vanstav's distinctive skills was easily transferable to the target company: their ability to optimize the manufacturing process. Consequently, Delta Hawk's productivity, which was one if its major weaknesses, would improve enormously. When all was said and done, Delta Hawk complemented best with Vanstav. The more he thought about it, the more advantages Gerd saw in this acquisition and he knew that he must not let it slip through his fingers.

Gerd once again gazed down at his worktable. His fingers, which were positioned over the region of Phoenix, crossed the map in a straight line to reach Italy. Acquiring Mossi offered different advantages. The first, and by no means the least, was the fact that he would be thumbing his nose at Guido Valli by grabbing hold of a large portion of the Italian market. Asserting himself on his rival's own territory was a juicy idea, especially after the latest failures he had endured on the other side of the world.

Vanstav would become co-leader in Italy! Mossi offered a second advantage: Mossi's products and Vanstav's complemented each other very well. The combined sales of their products should lead to a noticeable increase in the new group's turnover. This increase in sales would help them to obtain the expected return on investments made. Gerd Strunz was waiting for confirmation from his Italian team. The production experts were to establish to what extent the increase in production volumes would translate into economies of scale.

The last battles between Vanstav and A.M.I. in Asia had left their mark on Vanstav's CEO. The fight with A.M.I. was becoming suicidal. Beating the other at any price had become the leitmotif. Strunz now wanted to get off this deadly spiral. That was why the American acquisition was the most important one. It was motivated by rational, economic logic. On the other hand, Strunz was aware that the Italian bid was motivated in the first place by rivalry with A.M.I. The economic logic was secondary: besides, this acquisition would bring in less than Delta Hawk as far as long-term performance was concerned.

"We must succeed in the USA. That's the priority. We have to make a serious attempt in Italy. If that takeover bid fails, it won't be serious. Other opportunities will occur in Europe." Gerd Strunz was confident. His change of strategy was timely. In the future, he would let A.M.I. sink into the mud alone. "Strictly speaking, no, I will not let Guido Valli and A.M.I. go under: Peter, Olaf and myself will hasten the nosedive," he thought. He picked up his phone and called Peter Guff.

The outcomes

Mancini was tired, but happy. A.M.I. would control Mossi and they would have 100% ownership of the capital. The negotiations had been long and tricky. The Mossi executives, assisted by their advisers, had forced A.M.I. three times to revise its initial bid upwards. Guido Valli had been called in to help. He had taken part in the final days' negotiations. He had given the go-ahead to the price increases. A.M.I. would pay €370 million in several instalments. The financial, legal and tax experts had devised a complex arrangement to finance the operation and to optimize its fiscal aspects.

The price might appear too high. Not for Mancini, for you had to add an opportunity cost to the value of the target company and the synergies. In fact, A.M.I. would have been penalized in the long run, if certain competitors had acquired Mossi. The possible loss of market share justified the price increase.

Now back in his office after a few days' rest, Mancini was leafing through the economic journals his secretary had brought in to him. There were articles in the Italian dailies about the acquisition. Journalists mentioned how the two companies were complementary to justify their favourable stance on this merger. The A.M.I. communications department had done a good job in keeping the emphasis on the strategic aspects and not revealing the exact terms of the agreement. There were interviews with Guido Valli. In the interviews he had concentrated on the prospects for development that this merger offered. After the local press, Mancini read the international dailies. He could only find a few rare communiqués that mentioned the acquisition.

"The Americans aren't really bothered about what happens in other countries," he thought. "And yet it's European countries that dominate our industry."

A paragraph in the *Financial Times* suddenly caught his attention.

"Damn it!" he exclaimed. He jumped up and ran to his boss's office, still holding the newspaper. The personal assistant stopped him, informing him that the CEO was on the phone. Mancini waited. Two minutes later she told him that the phone call had finished. Mancini knocked and went in without waiting. Guido Valli was still hanging up the phone. He was livid. Mancini knew there was a problem.

"Are you all right, Mister Valli?"

Guido Valli looked up slowly at his deputy. He took a deep breath, sat up in his chair and said:

"Everything's fine. What's the matter, Mancini?"

"Look at the newspaper, Mister Valli. Vanstav has just acquired Delta Hawk! It's incredible! We suspected them of wanting to acquire Mossi; in fact, they've attacked on the other side of the Atlantic!"

"I know, Mancini. I've just found out. Leave me please. I need peace and quiet."

"But, Mister Valli, I don't understand. It's very important. They're going to leave us trailing in North America. We've got to work out how we can counterattack quickly."

"Mancini, get out now," Guido Valli yelled.

Objection!

Mossi denounced the contract less than two weeks after it had been ratified. A clause in the document guaranteed Mossi that it could pull out of the deal within a certain period if it was found that A.M.I. had flouted ethical rules during the bidding process. Mossi invoked this clause.

Just after the contract was signed, Peter Guff had had a long meeting with the Mossi directors, had supplied them with the evidence and had outlined Vanstav's strategy for resolving the problem. The directors asked him for time to think and promised that Vanstav would be informed of their decisions. Gerd Strunz and his close colleagues believed that the contract would be denounced. It was logical. The Mossi CEO informed Gerd Strunz that negotiations would be resumed. The three companies who had competed with A.M.I. in the last round were once again on the starting line.

"It's a wise choice," Strunz told him. "And you have to treat each candidate equally. We don't feel that you owe us anything, for you've helped us to clean up matters."

Vanstav therefore became a bidder again like the others. Perhaps they would win, perhaps they would lose. Whatever the outcome, Vanstav would still be a winner. It would take A.M.I. some time to get rid of its demons and recover. Mossi had issued a terse press release informing the public of its decision. Ten days later, the financial press published a paragraph under the heading "Appointments", announcing Guido Valli's resignation and his replacement by Mancini at the head of A.M.I. The action plan thought up one month earlier with Peter Guff and Olaf Spack had produced the results they had hoped for.

The plan and the evidence

Vanstav's trap had worked. Two days after the trap had been set, the net had closed and Peter had convened an urgent meeting with Gerd.

"Olaf announced our latest bid of €344 million for Mossi to our Italian team last Tuesday. Our man sent a message five hours later using his personal email address. His message mentioned a house measuring 344 square metres that he wanted to buy. Now, ten days ago, the same person sent a similar message to the same address, the only difference being that the house measured 328 square metres. At that time our bid was €328 million ... What a funny coincidence!"

Gerd Strunz was getting impatient.

"Peter, who's the traitor?"

"Urs Mayer."

Urs Mayer, head of communications! Gerd Strunz found it difficult to believe. And yet, this was what Peter had just told him.

"Peter, if we're talking about personal emails, how did you manage to read them?"

"Our network system of computers made the operation easy. Remember those hackers who managed to get into the files in the Pentagon and at NASA. Mayer is connected from his home to the Vanstav email system and to his own. I got into his computer via the Vanstav system and managed to gain access to his personal Internet account. The crafty devil had wiped all the messages he had received and sent, but he forgot to wipe his Internet history file that keeps a record of all his connections. This enabled me to read his emails."

"Say no more, Peter, network technology is beyond me. By the way, did you identify the person who received the messages from Mayer?"

Peter mentioned a name, but Gerd did not recognize it.

"That's not unusual," Peter said. "The address belongs to a user who got his connection from a free email provider. There is no check on identities, and the person must have supplied a fictitious name and address. If this person has been careful, we'll find it difficult to identify him. I'll keep looking. What are we going to do about Mayer?" Peter asked.

"Nothing. Nothing at all. We'll continue the discussions with Mossi and we'll keep Mayer in the team. Now, it's our turn to play. We hold all the cards; we've got to take advantage of that. Go and get Olaf and both of you come to my office."

When Peter Guff had left, Gerd slumped back in his chair and lit his pipe. Urs Mayer, head of communications for the last ten years! A mainstay of the company. Someone who excelled in his job. That was why, in each acquisition project, Gerd had put him in charge of internal and external communications strategy. But Urs Mayer was also a manager who had been languishing in his role for some years now. He was desperate for promotion, but Gerd believed that he did not have the necessary skills to take on a more important managerial role. Perhaps he had become embittered because he had been turned down for promotion?

Gerd Strunz was beginning to understand why he had lost out on certain takeover bids. Moreover, he had nearly always lost to A.M.I. It was clearly obvious that Mayer had been working on behalf of A.M.I. Strunz saw clearly what had been going on. There had been insider dealing. The recent battles had not been fought fairly. There was one thing they still needed to find out before they could stop the rules of the game being stretched: the identity of the contact or contacts in A.M.I. They had to be highly placed.

The arrival of his two lieutenants interrupted his thoughts. The three men spent two hours together refining their strategy and working out an action plan. First of all, the negotiations with Delta Hawk would have to remain top secret. The parallel discussions with Mossi would continue. The objective would be to raise the price as high as possible: in fact, it was obvious that, in Italy, A.M.I. would not let any competitor get hold of the target company. It would inform its Italian team, of which Urs Mayer was a member, of its successive bids. Peter Guff would continue monitoring the messages sent by the traitor and would try to track down the person they were being sent to.

As soon as Mossi had signed with A.M.I., Peter would show Urs Mayer's messages to the Mossi directors and tell them that Vanstav was going to expose the scandal. Gerd would force Urs Mayer to resign. Then he would tell the A.M.I. family shareholders about the incident and show them the messages. They would certainly react before the affair became public.

Urs Mayer made it easy for them. The Italian team were working around the clock on the dossier in offices that had been rented for the occasion. Olaf, who was with them in Italy, gave out some important information concerning their latest valuation of Mossi. Mayer could not use his laptop as he had left it at the hotel. Olaf kept an eye on him all the time. Mayer left the room to go to the toilet. Olaf followed him discreetly. He overheard Mayer phoning from an office that was next to the room they were working in. When Mayer went back to the team, Olaf picked up the phone, pressed "redial" and waited. The phone was answered. He heard a voice say: "Hello, Valli speaking ..." Olaf hung up at once.

Everything went according to plan: when the contract for the acquisition of Mossi by A.M.I. was signed, Gerd Strunz summoned Mayer. The latter confessed and left the company immediately. A.M.I.'s family shareholders were informed by Gerd Strunz, they called an extraordinary meeting of the board and sacked Guido Valli. He accepted entire responsibility for the affair. Competition in the takeover bids had now been cleaned up.

The extent of the damage in A.M.I.

Mancini was happy with his promotion, but he was now beginning to think about the task that lay ahead of him. The numerous acquisitions of recent years had increased A.M.I.'s debt by a considerable amount. Their South American and Asian businesses were losing money. Integration plans for the companies they had acquired in these regions were not far advanced, creating a doubt as to whether there would be a return to profit in the near future. In fact, the race to acquire, Guido Valli's obsession, had made him lose his head, both figuratively and literally. He had not taken the time to put in place an organization nor to choose people who could prepare for and manage these integrations. So, synergies were not being exploited.

A.M.I.'s lead in technology, once its strong point, had melted away. Diverting investment capital toward acquisitions had hurt research and development. Innovations were beginning to appear from small competitors. What partly reassured Mancini, was that the Vanstav product ranges were apparently experiencing the same problems of technical decline. The fight for leadership had weakened the two enemies. There would have to be a pause for reflection and an action plan would have to be drawn up to win back a competitive advantage.

Finally, the business world was wondering why Guido Valli had been pushed aside so abruptly. The employees also did not understand. Mancini would have to work out a communication strategy that would nip the crisis in the bud before it exploded into daylight. The poor financial results would be used to justify the sacking. The shareholders would support Mancini in his actions.

Guido Valli had left overnight. He had only removed his personal objects. Mancini walked over to the chessboard left behind by his old boss. "Guido Valli, black has won, you've been checkmated," he thought. "You had me fooled with your ability to work out your opponent's moves." In anger he swung a kick at the table. The chessmen scattered all over the carpet, the white king broke as it fell off and the "map of the world" chessboard cracked.

"It was all a facade," he reflected. "And now today, our company is paying the price." He pressed the intercom and called his assistant: "Maria, please have someone remove the chessboard from my office today."

2.2. COMBINING EGO AND GEO ...

Guido Valli lost his way in this dash for world supremacy. His personal ambition was more important than having a strategic plan for his company. His game of chess using the world as his personal chessboard served his cause more than his group's. Furthermore, he weakened his company by getting into debt and by neglecting to strengthen the firms he had acquired. I am going to use the story in Section 2.1 – "To conquer the world" – to examine the motives of top executives and the strategies of international firms. In brief, what are the real objectives behind foreign acquisitions?

Is there a problem of dyslexia?

To listen to the arguments put forward by top executives, you would think that every acquisition corresponded to some strategic plan that promised a better future, thanks to synergies that are supposed to exist between the buyers and the target company, or thanks to a reduction in the risks linked to breaking into a new industry. If we consider the case of foreign acquisitions, which have increased noticeably in recent years, we always hear the same justifications. Who has not seen or heard messages such as: "this acquisition will give us a bigger share of the international market" or "thanks to this acquisition, we will be able to extend our technological advance to this part of the world"? So, very quickly, it becomes a question of geographical considerations – the "geo" in the title of this chapter – when an executive is explaining why he is acquiring a foreign company. Yet, examination of the facts leads us to wonder about the real motives of top executives. Could their egos be more important than the geo? Could some of them be dyslexic?

Personal interest and the interest of the group

Frankly, if you are a top executive, what better way to flatter your ego and look after your own personal interests than acquiring another company? An acquisition is an important investment and a leap forward. The size of your company instantly increases. Your strategic position may be greatly improved. It's brilliant! Thanks to the acquisition, you have become the manager of a more powerful group. And, at the same time, you do not have to give up any of the power you already have.[1] Your pride is flattered: you are the phoenix of your industry. The people around you respect you more. You become increasingly well known and respected on the outside. You think: "Good, I'll have to find another company to acquire soon." You think about Edgar Bronfman Jr, the boss of Seagram who acquired Universal Studios ...

---

[1] If we follow this reasoning to its logical conclusion, you should avoid mergers if you think you will lose power ...

Researchers investigating the subject of corporate governance have studied this type of opportunist behaviour. This deals with the relationship between executives and shareholders. It can be defined as the ways in which those who provide companies with financial resources are assured of a return on their investment (Shleifer and Vishny, 1989). In line with this definition, most of the research was focused on the behaviour of executives and the methods of controlling these executives that shareholders could and should exert. Let's make a detour to have a look at this research.

Although executives are obliged to serve the best interests of the shareholders, there is still scope for them to display some opportunism. In fact, they have some discretionary powers that enable them to get round, avoid or neutralize the control systems that the shareholders have put in place. From these ideas has come the theory of executive entrenchment; this theory describes executives' propensity for preserving or increasing their discretionary power and the energy they expend in doing so. Charreaux (1996) has distinguished two entrenchment strategies: in-house entrenchment and external career.

The *in-house entrenchment strategy* sets out to make you indispensable as the head of your company. Executives achieve this aim by making idiosyncratic investments, by manipulating information or by developing a unique ability to control financial or strategic resources. In this way, the ability to make an acquisition may be recognized by shareholders as a specific skill the executive has. The latter will turn this to good account: he will make himself indispensable for the smooth running of the business; he may increase his discretionary power or negotiate an increase in his remuneration.

Not every executive seeks to maintain his position within the company. He may also, through his deeds as the head of an organization, seek to increase his standing in the market for top executives: this is the *external career strategy*. That's how Hirshleifer (1993) saw things: the executive is seeking to enhance his reputation as a competent manager. In order to achieve this objective, he manipulates information concerning his investment policy. Three types of manipulation are conceivable: favour short-term performance in order to enhance his reputation; communicate favourable information as soon as possible and hold back unfavourable information; or even model his behaviour on that of renowned executives.

Studies carried out in the USA have also shown that the control mechanisms put in place by shareholders were not always effective. For example, researchers have associated the propensity for buying companies with a method of remunerating executives that is linked to the evolution of the company's turnover. Who would not be tempted?

In brief, acquisitions are bound to flatter the executive's ego and can sometimes serve his own personal interests. Is this regrettable and harmful? No. The initial premise that there was always a negative side to this sort of opportunism has been replaced by a more balanced vision of things, one that recognizes that individualistic behaviour may also serve the shareholders' interests. Thus, Castanias and Helfat (1992) believe that the creation of personal managerial rents could be perceived by shareholders as a way of rewarding the executive for his ability to carry out profitable projects.

To conclude, the roles played by ego and personal interest are legitimate; if they combine with the collective interest, they can underpin a takeover bid. Long live the ego, but without the egoism!

Variety of geostrategic objectives

Personal objectives must therefore converge with a strategic project for the company. Executives, whether they are players or followers in today's huge exercise in globalization, have to confront new realities on a worldwide scale. The growing size of organizations and the quest for market share in the international arena gives food for thought about the place that acquisitions occupy in strategies and about the ability of executives to drive the process from the phase of hopes to the phase of achievements.

As it happens, a large number of industries are today either global, on their way to becoming global or transnational. The competitive game consists in creating for yourself an attractive strategic positioning on a scale that involves several countries. Industries are distinguished by the extent of their integration and coordination forces, like the existence of economies of scale or the predominance of a worldwide customer base. These forces encourage corporations to internationalize and to work out global strategies. At the same time industries are also distinguished by the extent of their localization forces, especially in situations where the distribution networks differ from country to country or where each country has different norms that apply. When a product or a service needs to be adapted for each national market, differentiated strategies have to be worked out according to the countries concerned. Each industry therefore possesses its own mix of forces (Atamer and Calori, 1993).

We talk of *global* or worldwide industry when the integration and coordination forces are strong and the localization forces are weak; in such a sector, the quest for world supremacy guides the strategic reflection. An industry is labelled *multi-domestic* or *multi-local* when pressures to integrate are weak, whereas the localization forces are strong. Such an industry is favourable to the development of differentiated national strategies: there is little to be gained from standardizing products. Finally, industries where both types of forces are exerted simultaneously are called *cross-border* or *mixed industries*. Here, the players can choose between a global strategy, a cross-border strategy or a local adaptation strategy: either (1) they sell the same product everywhere, or (2) they find a balance between standardization for a group of countries and local adaptation of the product, or (3) they adapt their products to suit each country.

This detour – presented in a simplified manner – to explain the basic foundations of international strategy was essential in order to understand the stakes involved in acquisition manoeuvres abroad. In fact, according to the type of strategy implemented, the acquisitions contribute to the implementation of different objectives. When the buyer is pursuing a global strategy, the acquisition of a company in his own sector of activity is aimed at strengthening his competitiveness worldwide. The favoured targets are those that will offer a conspicuous gain in world market share or that will help to eliminate a relatively weak spot in certain parts of the world. At the other extreme, when the corporation is developing a multi-local strategy, an acquisition abroad is aimed at building a new competitive position in the country or countries where the target company operates. In fact, since the buyer is not looking to take advantage of any eventual integration and coordination forces, the targets likely to interest him are those that benefit from an attractive positioning, deeply rooted in the specific local character of the country or countries.

These differences in strategy have strong repercussions on the acquisition process. Not only do they affect the selection of targets, which is made according to different criteria, but they also affect the valuation, the fixing of a price and the implementation of the merger. Figure 2.1 illustrates these differences.

Let's examine first of all the case of the buyer who is pursuing a global strategy. Exploiting integration and coordination forces means exploiting synergies. After the takeover, a large part of the value will be created by sharing resources or by transferring skills between companies. Therefore, an assessment of the synergies is necessary. It will be integrated into the calculation of a maximum price that the buyer will accept to pay to get control of the target company. Consequently, the companies will work closely together during the phase of achievements. They will have to exploit synergies, and achieve the levels of consolidation and standardization that correspond to the assumptions made in their global strategy. Functional redundancy will pose a problem: they will certainly have to consider parting with some executives and middle managers. They will also have to build one organization from the two previous ones. The acquisition of V.L.S.I. by Philips Semiconductors in 1999 is a good

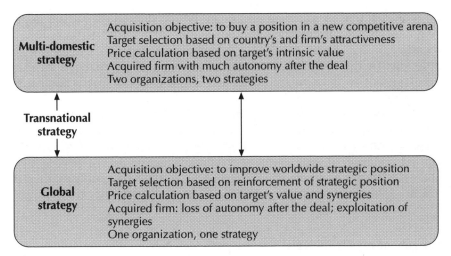

Figure 2.1   Geostrategy and the acquisition process.

example of this scenario. In this global segment of the electronics industry, the Dutch company Philips acquired the Californian company in order to strengthen its areas of competence, to improve its coverage of the world market and to increase its access to other types of customers. Synergies were examined very carefully. The directors quickly realized that they would have to absorb the whole of V.L.S.I. into their own organization. New managers were appointed; most of the duplicate posts were abolished. An integration plan was drawn up to interweave the structures and exploit the synergies. The merger was completed for the most part in six months.

The buyer who is pursuing a multi-local strategy will proceed in a different way. The valuation will concern above all an assessment of the value represented by the target company. In fact, any synergies to be exploited are nonexistent. Negotiation of the price to pay revolves around the assumptions made about this value. Since there are no synergies, it will be in the companies' interests to be managed independently: each one will adapt to its local market conditions. In fact, there will be very few redundancies, as nearly every post will be necessary in each country. It might seem ridiculous. However, this is what the economy hotels group, Accor, did, when it moved into the USA on acquiring the Motel 6 chain. Even if a few transfers of management skills were possible, the American chain still retained a lot of autonomy in the way it was run. Consolidation with the European economy hotel chain, Formule 1, was inappropriate because it would have generated more costs than benefits. Indeed, the concept of economy hotels does not have the same meaning for a French person as for an American. Where the French person might be happy with automated operations, the American would prefer to have a member of staff at his service. In addition, construction methods were different. In the end, it was better to let each chain manage its own development in its own territories where its concept was attractive to local people.

To sum up, these examples illustrate the variety of objectives underpinning foreign acquisitions. There is not one international strategy; there are geostrategies (i.e., ways of deploying your resources on the map of the world in relation to your choice of strategic direction and to geographical characteristics[2]). So, there are various ways of choosing countries, then of acquiring local targets and combining them with your own company.

The role of the geostrategist

The large number of mergers and acquisitions in certain industries has led people to speak of a wave of concentration. This conclusion is subject to caution. Concentration may indeed be taking place in the telecommunications and aviation industries, but it is not evident in the pharmaceutical industry where, nevertheless, there have been a number of mergers in recent years: Warner-Lambert and Pfizer, SmithKline Beecham and Glaxo Wellcome, Astra and Zeneca, Hoechst Marion Roussel and Rhone Poulenc, Pharmacia Upjohn and Monsanto, Ciba and Sandoz. At the end of 1998, the turnovers of the 20 biggest pharmaceutical groups ranged between US$10.7 billion and US$3.7 billion. The whole industry is made up of numerous players, none of whom has a clear domination. The new group GlaxoSmithKline has a market share of around 7% (cf., the Internet site gsk.com). The growth in size of the big companies has not necessarily been accompanied by a contingent increase in market share. The size of the markets served can also grow as well, as the pharmaceutical industry clearly demonstrates. On the other hand, because national barriers are now disappearing, we are obliged to calculate market share on a continental or global scale. As the cake increases in size, many acquisitions are

---

[2] The concept of geostrategy is used in reference to the work of P.M. Gallois in *Géopolitique – Les Voies de la Puissance*, Plon, Paris, 1990. Talking about geopolitics, the author explains the new premise on which his discipline rests: "If nature influences life, it is no longer through its innate character, but through the effect of the transformations that man has made it undergo" (p. 14). Since it was man who put up barriers to free exchange, since human geography influences the strategic attractivity of countries, we have deliberately borrowed the concept of geostrategy to characterize the thinking of executives at the head of multinational companies.

aimed at preserving market share that was obtained on more limited territories. Here we are seeing a battle against erosion. Where some people talk about international offensives, we should really be talking about defensive manoeuvres.

Whether or not there is a concentration, mergers and acquisitions have created groups gathering together tens or hundreds of thousands of employees. Such sizes mean that management principles have to be reviewed. The executives of a big multinational group can no longer manage an individual, a team or even one site. They manage a portfolio of businesses (business units), choose the direction of strategy, work out organization principles, react to the consolidated financial data, manage relationships with shareholders and banks, represent the company in the outside world. Employee V doing W, on site X, in country Y, at post Z becomes just a number in a wide population. His position is similar to that of the Roman legionnaire in the time of Julius Caesar: 5th legion, 3rd cohort, 2nd century, 1st contubernium. The company's top executives appear inaccessible. Even if they multiply their site visits, the large number of units means that they will only visit factory X once every three or four years. In addition, these big bosses do not speak employee V's language. How far we have come from the days when the identity of the company was constructed around the personality of the boss!

This question of distances has consequences for the conduct of acquisitions. Like a state or an army, the executive needs deputies, representatives of his power, closer to the ground. In places where local strategic adaptation is necessary, the power of decision-making or the choices of development are worth delegating to the level of the country or the geographical region. The top executive is therefore no longer directly involved with national strategies. He relies on other people to relay decisions and information. Consequently, some local acquisitions do not concern him anymore! They are decided on and managed at a lower hierarchical level. Top management, however, deals with other acquisitions, those that have a strong influence on the evolution of their portfolio of businesses. But whether they are local or worldwide, all these transactions mobilize the same internal resources: for example, the acquisitions department which gathers together financial, legal and tax experts, who specialize in this type of operation; or, for example, environmental protection experts who carry out a diagnosis of the industrial sites. If decision-making powers have been clearly established for each transaction envisaged, certain rare resources need to be shared. In fact, one of top management's essential tasks consists in putting in place an organization and methods that will make it easy to mobilize experts at various levels of the hierarchy in many different places. It is an eminently complex task if you wish to avoid duplication of resources within the structure. But it is a task that will decide if you are capable of reacting quickly to seize acquisitions opportunities. For acquisitions mean pressures of time.

Ego, geo and ... game of go

The desire to acquire is part of a strategic plan. When it is not perverted by an outsize ego, this plan corresponds to a choice of strategic orientations and methods of development that are supposed to create value for the shareholders, indeed for the other stakeholders in the organization. Creation of value for the shareholder is often understood to mean a short-term profit. However, the study of transactions carried out by large international groups suggests a different objective: the construction of the potential to create value in the long term. Facing his map of the world, the top executive puts down his pawns and examines those of his opponent. If some acquisitions immediately strengthen competitiveness, others represent the purchase of positions that could become strategic in the more distant future. When Lafarge acquired the British company, Redland, at the end of 1997, Bertrand Collomb, CEO of Lafarge, himself worked on this dossier. Indeed, the takeover of Redland, purchased for 15.9 billion francs, was a logical extension of their portfolio of businesses. On the other hand, when Lafarge acquired some cement works in the ex-Soviet republics or in the emerging countries of Asia for a relatively modest sum, the objective was different. When the local economy becomes more favourable, if it ever does, Lafarge will already be occupying the terrain and will be ready to take advantage of its investment. Following the example of military reasoning, some places are worth taking in order not to let the enemy set up there. It would be too difficult to dislodge them afterwards. The big cement manufacturers are watching out for privatizations in Egypt, are analysing opportunities in India and are awaiting impatiently the opening up of the vast Chinese market. The game of go, with its strategies of encirclement, with its taking up of positions, its offensive and defensive reasoning, symbolizes the thinking on strategic development. Acquisitions are pawns to be played, sometimes for immediate benefits, sometimes to gain long-term benefits.

Summary

Cross-border acquisitions are part of various strategic plans, for the well-being of the corporation and/or its CEO, thus combining ego with the geo. Working out a clear objective nevertheless remains essential, because the directions chosen will influence the design of the acquisition process. Dyslexia, when all is said and done, is not a problem ... except for those who, like Guido Valli, lose sight of the interests of the company that employs them.

Chapter 3

Choosing the right pilots

3.1. STORY: THE GOLD NUGGET

Around the table, the executives were silent. Michael Edertour was shouting loudly:

"Good grief! Can anyone tell me why we can't get into Chrysler?"

You could have heard a pin drop.

"This was one of the priorities we defined together two years ago. What's stopping us? Our products? The efforts of our competitors? Our relations with their purchasers?"

The Paint Inc. CEO's voice reverberated around the meeting room. Alicia Dupont, the marketing director, spoke:

"We did everything possible, but we need to adapt our product range. Chrysler today wants to use powder paint for certain types of priming or finish on its vehicles. And you know very well that we've got a very poor grasp of this technology."

"What's more, Mister Edertour, there is also a risk that we'll lose markets with other manufacturers if we can't offer them powder paint," added Lucas Banon, the sales director.

"To sum up," the chairman concluded, "you're telling me that our know-how is out of date and that our future is threatened. Thank you, ladies and gentlemen, I'm looking for solutions and you respond by outlining the problems. I need ideas for heaven's sake!"

The board meeting ended with these exchanges. As he was leaving the room, Lucas Banon addressed Alicia Dupont sharply:

"You should have told him about Core Paint."

"It wasn't the right moment. You saw how angry he was!"

"Well! We're going to have a very happy Christmas if he doesn't change ..."

A week later, the company was celebrating Christmas at a cocktail party for all 600 employees. Michael Edertour was in a good mood; he thanked his employees for their work during the past year and wished them all a happy Christmas. Alicia Dupont went up to him and gave him a glass of champagne.

"Merry Christmas, Mister Edertour!"

"Thank you, Alicia. And the same to you."

"Thank you. I know I'm changing the subject, but I'd like to talk to you a minute about our discussion concerning Chrysler and the powder paint. I may have the solution."

"Good grief, this is hardly the right moment!"

"My solution can't wait. Just think about all our customers who want powder paint tomorrow, and who will turn to our competitors for it; just think about all these people you see here, smiling, with a drink in their hands, and who, tomorrow, you will be obliged to fire; just think ..."

"Okay, Alicia. Just tell me what you have to say. Let's go over to the corner of the room where we we'll be able to talk in peace."

Michael walked across the room, smiling and nodding to his employees. Alicia followed him, under the astonished and suspicious looks of employees who had moved aside to let the chairman get past. Alone in the corner of the room, the two of them talked in hushed voices, watched discreetly by a number of people who had now got over their astonishment ...

"The solution to our problem is called Core Paint."

"Good heavens, what are you on about? They're our biggest competitor in this country."

"I know that."

"I don't get it. What are you trying to tell me?"

"It's simple, I think all our problems would be solved if we formed an alliance with Core Paint."

"What the devil are you suggesting?"

"Mister Edertour, Core Paint has enjoyed strong growth since it started making powder paint *and* it has got into Chrysler! It's a golden opportunity for us!"

"Listen, Alicia. It's getting late, and I have the feeling that some of the employees are getting suspicious, we'll discuss it again next Monday. That'll give us both some time to think about your idea. It might not be so daft after all."

"Not so daft, not so daft ... it's a brilliant idea!" Alicia grumbled to herself as Michael walked away.

The following Monday Alicia walked into Michael's office.

"Good morning, Alicia, have a seat. Before we start, I have to say that I wasn't very happy with the way you accosted me the other evening. As you are aware, my wife knows quite a few of our employees and she got to hear about it. She exploded in a fit of jealousy at the weekend! So, from now on, don't corner me like that in public again!"

"But, it was you who suggested that we talk alone in ..."

"That's enough! Just don't do it again, that's all!"

"But, ..."

"I said that's enough! Now, calm down and tell me about your idea."

Alicia sighed. What a boor, she thought. And what dishonesty. To say that I did all that because I was interested in him. She took a deep breath. Michael waited for her to start speaking, not only in order to find out what she was going to say, but also to make sure that she had indeed changed the subject of the conversation and to thus extract himself from the mess he was getting himself into.

"First of all, you still want to get into Chrysler in spite of all our attempts and failures these past two years. Second, you want to manufacture powder paint. I can see only one solution: acquire or form a partnership with a company that sells powder paint to Chrysler. These last few months I have been carrying out an in-depth study of our competitors. Only one company satisfies these two conditions and is at the same time of a suitable size for Paint Inc. If we can afford to, the ideal solution would be to acquire Core Paint, otherwise we could propose an alliance with them."

"It's an interesting idea. I had time to think about it over the weekend, as my wife decided to go off to the country. We hadn't thought about an acquisition, but why not? At first sight Core Paint certainly looks attractive. Of course, we'll have to investigate more thoroughly to find out what their real potential is. However, before we go any further, there is one problem: as far as I know, Core Paint is not up for sale ..."

"I'll answer that by quoting our financial director, Gaston Febura: 'Everything is for sale, it's just a question of price.' I've made enquiries about Core Paint: they are a third of our weight, in turnover and in staff numbers; they are experiencing strong growth in their one and only segment: automobile paints. The boss, Bernard Bloq, along with his family circle, holds 100% of the capital. And I've heard that he's having some difficulty in financing Core Paint's growth, because the other family shareholders are not willing to reinvest in the company. In fact, he may be thinking about opening up his capital to new partners."

"Well done, Alicia, good work! I can see you've started exploring this avenue seriously," Michael said, to win back Alicia's trust and to make her forget about the start of the conversation. "This acquisition would seem a priori like a good idea, but we still have to prove that it's feasible and to check our first impressions. I suggest that we work as follows: I'll put you officially in charge of this dossier. Work together with Gaston Febura, for you're going to need him. Take, let's say, three weeks to carry out four analyses: first of all, a strategic diagnosis of Core Paint; second, a financial valuation of the target and any synergies there are, so that we can calculate how much the acquisition might cost us; third, a first analysis of how we can finance such an operation; finally, a check on how predisposed Bernard Bloq is to opening up his capital. I'll talk to Gaston Febura about the project; we'll need his help in order to judge the economic impact of such an acquisition on our company. Give me regular updates on how your investigations are progressing. And above all, the two of you must work as discreetly as possible! No one here or on the outside must get wind of our idea. Oh sorry! Of *your* idea."

Michael got up and held out his hand.

"Good heavens, Alicia, if this project comes to something, we'll both be setting off on a crazy, new adventure!" the CEO exclaimed in his stentorian voice.

"Talking about discretion, you should avoid saying things like that at the top of your voice. I don't think your wife would appreciate it," Alicia retorted in a somewhat resentful voice as she left his office. She walked past his personal assistant, who looked shocked, and moved quickly toward the stairs that led to the floor below, with a sardonic smile on her face.

"What character, but what a woman!" Michael thought as he relaxed in his chair. "Her idea is excellent. We've amassed a lot of cash these last few years: financing it shouldn't be a problem. Acquiring Core Paint will give us a presence in all of the country's car manufacturers and access to all of today's technologies. We would be the undisputed leader! OK, let's not get carried away, we still haven't bought anything. On the one hand, we've got to make sure that Bernard Bloq is willing to sell, and I'm not sure about that. On the other hand, we've never made any acquisitions before; I'll have to find out how to go about it."

The phone rang, interrupting his thoughts. Michael picked it up. It was his wife. He sighed. She wanted to know who had been in his office ten minutes ago. He uttered another sigh . . .

Negotiations

"Okay, I agree to sell on the terms we've already discussed."

Michael felt relieved on this 3rd March. After three months of negotiation, Bernard Bloq had finally agreed.

Alicia and Gaston, assisted by a consulting firm, had made a general diagnosis of Core Paint, and had then studied the complementarities between the two companies. Overall, Core Paint was well organized, well managed and well positioned in its market. A little jewel. The target was worth between €40 million and €46 million, according to the hypotheses and the valuations they had made. When synergies were taken into account, they could pay up to €52 million without running the risk of weakening the buyer. Simulation exercises had been carried out using information that Alicia had obtained from published sources. Of course, these needed to be supported by direct investigation inside the target company.

The consultants had contacted Core Paint and had held discussions with Bernard Bloq, convincing him to meet Michael Edertour to discuss an eventual merger. At the first meeting the air had been frosty, both outside and inside the Core Paint meeting room. In fact, Bernard Bloq now discovered Michael's true intentions: "merger" meant control of Core Paint by Paint Inc.! In addition, Bernard did not like Michael, who came across as very haughty and sure of himself, and had squeezed his fingers when he had shaken hands with him. That was why he quickly put an end to the meeting, indicating that his company was not for sale. As he saw his visitors out, Bernard Bloq was still rubbing the fingers on his right hand and thinking: "if, one day I do have to sell my company to these jerks, they'll pay a high price, a very high price indeed ..."

And then the idea of selling had started to gain ground in Bernard's mind. He knew that the survival of his company was at stake, for in today's markets it was the biggest companies who were at an advantage. They needed to grow quickly. Core Paint needed an injection of capital, but the minority family shareholders wanted to withdraw their participation as quickly as possible. He had just been involved in a sordid squabble with his family-in-law over an inheritance, so it did not surprise him that they wanted to withdraw their capital from the firm. Bernard was also becoming exhausted in his role at the head of the company, a role he had taken over from his father-in-law. The company was doing well, was developing, but he felt that he was just going round in circles. Since the squabble over the inheritance, his relationship with his wife had deteriorated and she had left him. They had no children. All the more reason to have a change of scenery.

In the end, Bernard decided to study Paint Inc.'s proposition. Ignoring his personal animosity toward the top man, he accepted that Paint Inc. was a good company, the leader in this country in automobile paints. He quickly understood the interest that his company presented for Paint Inc.: the market with Chrysler, the "powder" technology. He also realized that any merger would come at a price for some of his employees. In fact, both companies had some product lines that were similar and they worked mainly with the same customers. Consequently, certain salesforces and production teams would have to be merged and some administrative posts would be abolished. They would not be able to avoid redundancies.

Bernard Bloq then turned his attention to Paint Inc.'s capital structure. He noted that the company was a majority-owned subsidiary of a large foreign group, a conglomerate with diverse interests. However, Paint

Inc. was managed autonomously, because its core activity was not part of its head office's priorities.

These realizations stirred his imagination. He decided to contact his investment bank. When the consultants returned to the attack a month after the first meeting, the idea of selling had gained more ground inside Bernard Bloq's mind. He agreed to meet Michael and his team again. With a smile on his face, he greeted them warmly this time. He shook Michael's hand, squeezing his fingers in the process. His smile stealthily turned into a grin tainted with a little cruelty. Then he introduced his banker and agreed to enter into negotiations with the Paint Inc. team without pre-judging the outcome. As proof of his goodwill, he agreed to let Paint Inc. visit sites, meet his top managers and examine a certain number of files. A document stipulating the objectives and the conditions under which Paint Inc. could examine internal information was signed a few days later.

Assisted by his banker, Bernard Bloq estimated the intrinsic value of his company to be between €45 million and €52 million. When synergies were added to this, he could reasonably expect to sell for between €50 million and €57 million. As it was rare to find acquisition targets in this line of business, Bernard decided not to sell for less than €59 million. His banker did not agree with him on this. Bernard justified his position by relating a story about handshakes that left his banker completely mystified.

As he left the second meeting Michael had mixed feelings. He was happy with Bernard Bloq's change in attitude; nevertheless, he could not understand why this jerk had squeezed his fingers. As soon as he was back in his office, he launched the final investigation inside Core Paint. Michael was delighted: as his friends had suggested, he was going to be able to conduct his own "due diligence" investigation in order to ascertain the target's strengths and weaknesses. He had also taken great pleasure in shutting Bloq up; he had concluded the last meeting with a scathing remark: "My dear sir, I don't think we'll have any problems reaching an agreement if the due diligence investigation comes up with all the guarantees we want and if your company satisfies all our deal-killers.[1]" Bernard Bloq had sat there, dumbfounded.

The due diligence investigation began the following month and lasted three weeks. It focused on two themes: an extensive examination of Core Paint's accounts and a diagnosis of research and development that focused on the protection of innovations. The hypotheses produced by the first simulation exercises were lowered slightly and brought the value of the company down to a sum between €46 million and €51 million. Negotiations began in a country hotel. Sometimes Bernard would bluntly

---

[1] Criteria that must be satisfied in order for negotiations to be pursued.

refuse an offer; sometimes he would ask for time to think. Worn out and irritated at having to put so much energy into these negotiations, Michael and his team pitched their fourth proposition at €51 million. Bernard refused, on the grounds that they had not considered the opportunity cost. Michael asked him what this opportunity cost was. Bernard Bloq, smiling radiantly, gave him a very clear explanation: he pointed out the interest that Core Paint might present for another competitor who, thanks to this acquisition, could become the market leader. Michael then called for an investment bank to break the deadlock. So, an investment banker joined the negotiations. The discussions focused on the price and its justification. The banker did not approve of the methods they had adopted, which he believed had little structure to them. But he accepted that they would have to take into account an opportunity cost. From that moment the bid increased to €54 million.

Bernard Bloq then felt that he would not get any more. The people on the other side were clearly getting tired. In addition, the atmosphere among Core Paint employees was morose. The many visits by people from Paint Inc. had helped to create a lot of uncertainty in their minds, which their boss's reassuring words could not dispel.

Bernard then decided not to hold out for the €59 million. On the 3rd March at 12 : 00, two days after Michael Edertour's banker had joined the negotiating table, he accepted the offer of €54 million under certain conditions that had been laid down a week earlier.

Final negotiations

The investment banker then asked about these conditions of which he had no knowledge.

"We agreed on two conditions. The first is that I want to have a clause inserted in the contract stipulating that the buyer cannot under any circumstances make one of my employees redundant for financial reasons during the next two years. The second condition is that they find me a management post in Paint Inc.'s parent company. And, talking of which, I still haven't received a response."

Michael's banker was completely dumbfounded; having arrived in the middle of the negotiations, he was now discovering that his client had made moral commitments to the seller without telling him. He then took Michael aside and asked for more information. He also wanted to know if they could have further discussions on the terms of this oral agreement. Michael was exhausted, but happy to have closed the deal and, despite his anxiety at the sum he has going to pay out, he put an end to the banker's questions by refusing to reopen negotiations. The banker pointed out that he would not be held responsible for any possible consequences of Michael's decision, and he left in a furious mood.

Once he was back in his office, Michael checked out his contacts at head office. There were two posts to fill that corresponded to Bernard Bloq's profile. He immediately had this information passed on to the latter. Then he sank back into his chair and put his feet on the desk.

"Good grief, it's the first time I've felt so relieved!"

Michael had sweated a lot these past weeks and was satisfied to have concluded matters. Fear, joy, anxiety, suffering, surprise and anger: he had experienced them all in such a short time, going from one extreme to the other. He was still anxious about the consequences. If the acquisition bore fruit, it would be "banco"; if it failed, it could be a catastrophe. Worn out, he fell asleep in his chair.

The door suddenly opening awakened him. His wife stood in front of him, with an astounded look on her face.

"So, Michael, this is how you work? Lazy so-and-so, you've been telling me yarns with your so-called project that kept you working night and day ..."

"But, dear, ..."

His wife turned around and slammed the door as she left the office in a fury.

A period of change

Bernard was sitting comfortably in his huge, leather chair. He had lit his pipe. He was admiring Paris through the plate glass window in his office on the 35th floor of a tower in La Défense. Six months after the signature of the contract, he had just taken up his new post in the Paris head office of the American parent company. It had taken some time to find this job, but Bernard had no regrets. The fact that he spoke French, combined with the experience he had gained as head of Core Paint, had finally got him the job. When he had arrived that morning, he had received a warm welcome. There was already a sign on his office door that read in French and in English: "Bernard Bloq, European Key Accounts Manager". The office was spacious and equipped with the information system he had requested.

"My second life," he thought. "I love change. The unknown may be scary, but it's also exciting."

Of course, the fortune he had made by selling his company had helped him to face the change serenely. The lights were going on all over Paris. Bernard was enjoying the spectacle.

"The old humdrum routine of everyday life, that's all finished with now; a bit of fresh air will do me the world of good. And then, with a bit of luck, I'll find another wife. I'm about to start a new life far from my ex-wife and the Core Paint shareholders."

He rubbed the back of his right hand with his left hand unconsciously. This habit had started during the sales negotiations. "I hope my employees understood. I did take every precaution to safeguard their futures."

The Core Paint employees were fine. Disorientated when the sale of the company was announced, they had been angry with their old boss. However, the period of uncertainty was followed by a period of reassurance. In fact, the new CEO had delivered a speech in which he had convinced them of his ambition to develop the company. They now worked for the undisputed national leader in automobile paints. In addition, their jobs were safe. Consequently, they could look to the future serenely and could continue working using the "good old methods" of the past. In any case, their counterparts at Paint Inc. were not looking to cooperate.

As for Michael, he had a lot of problems. Each day brought its worries. Yesterday, a customer had called to denounce a contract. Apparently, certain of Core Paint's traditional customers did not like the takeover. Fortunately, Chrysler had not protested against the acquisition. Today, employees who worked at Paint Inc. before the merger had given notice of strike action. They were worried about the integration process: according to them, there was bound to be redundancies because of the existence of duplicate posts in management, purchasing, production and sales. And, according to the contractual commitments made at the time of the acquisition, it would not be Core Paint employees who would be made redundant. On top of all that, Michael had to recruit someone very quickly to replace Lucas Banon, his sales director, who had resigned. It would not be an easy task to replace someone as talented as Lucas. Alicia Dupont had been off on sick leave for two weeks. And then Gaston Febura was suffering from stress: he blamed the acquisition for creating an imbalance in the company's books, for, in the end, they had had to incur a large debt in order to finance the operation. So, the problems were piling up. And even his wife, whom he had managed to calm down these past weeks, was now complaining about the amount of time he was spending at the office, to the detriment of his family. She would not believe that he was actually working!

Michael was weary. "Good grief! If I had only known …" he thought, unconsciously rubbing the back of his right hand with his left hand …

3.2. IS THERE A PILOT IN THE ACQUISITION?

At first sight, the misadventures of Michael Edertour, the Paint Inc. boss, look like alchemy gone haywire: How can you turn a gold nugget into lead? The Core Paint jewel, which looked wonderful from a distance, turned out to bring nothing but trouble once it had been acquired. If Core Paint changed little, acquiring it created localized difficulties for the buyer.

A superficial analysis would lead you to think that Michael Edertour ought to have refused the conditions of sale imposed on him by his target. However, we need to remember that Paint Inc.'s competitiveness was deteriorating, that they had to acquire technological know-how in order to safeguard their future and that potential targets were apparently few and far between. So, it was in Michael's interest to act in order to maintain his company's competitiveness.

The range of potential solutions was, however, not studied. From the moment his colleague Alicia Dupont suggested Core Paint to him, Michael Edertour concentrated on this particular acquisition. Perhaps there were other choices? The acquisition of a target company represents an investment plan that ought to be compared systemically with other possible investments: buying a licence, an alliance, R&D development, other targets to buy, ... This sort of comparison would be all the more effective if it were being made regularly throughout the phase of hopes: since the price and the conditions of a sale evolve as knowledge of the target improves and negotiations progress, so the profits expected from the investment fluctuate with time. In referring to an alternative solution at regular intervals, the buyer can judge the wisdom of his plan at various stages of the negotiations.

Let's work on the assumption that acquiring Core Paint was seen as "the best solution". The real question then becomes: How do you negotiate the acquisition of a target when you are in a position of dependency, that is to say, when this acquisition is critical for defending the buyer's strategic position? Core Paint can live without Paint Inc., but Paint Inc. would have a better life with Core Paint at its side. Michael Edertour was negotiating from a position of relative weakness. He accepted the unfavourable conditions that contributed to creating problems within Paint Inc. Could he have avoided it? If the answer is yes, then he did not conduct the preliminary stages very skilfully. If the answer is no, then he should have prepared his company better to confront the post-acquisition difficulties. Whatever the answer, there is still a problem linked to how the acquisition process is conducted and to what the role of the pilot is. Hence our slightly provocative question in the title of this chapter: Is there a pilot in the acquisition?

In this section I am going to discuss the choice of pilots in relation to the acquisition process, then to reflect on methods of organizing and ways of working that seem appropriate to conducting the process effectively.

Piloting the hopes

Studying the target and negotiating the conditions of the merger make up the traditional stages of the journey that leads to an acquisition. They require skills in strategy, finance, law, taxation and negotiation that are rarely possessed by one single person. In fact, the phase of hopes is generally conducted by a team of people, including in-house experts and external consultants: investment banks, audit experts, law firms, advisers on strategy, on organization or on human resources. If need be, experts in environmental protection, in production, in marketing, or in information systems can be added ... The list is far from exhaustive.

There are at least two reasons the person in charge, who will oversee and organize the work of these experts, needs to be chosen carefully. The first one was put forward by Jemison and Sitkin (1987) in their research into managing the process. One major difficulty encountered by buyers lies in the fact that getting an overall picture of an acquisition project is a very complex undertaking. As the tasks are divided up between a large number of people, each one working on his own objective, the buyer's top management only receives partial information and analyses that it has to put together and integrate into an overall picture. For only this overall picture will enable them to evaluate the wisdom of the strategic plan. This dividing up of the tasks is necessary: since the buyer is experiencing a situation in which information is very scarce, it is in his interests to examine the analyses thoroughly in order to obtain the fullest possible information about the target company. On the other hand, the pressures of time, another characteristic of the process, mean that negotiations start before this overall picture is obtained. There is an increasing momentum to close the deal (Jemison and Sitkin, 1987). So, the buyer needs a pilot to coordinate actions, to summarize, to encourage the teams, to manage the pressures and to report the progress of the project to his managers.

The second reason for appointing a project leader is to do with the problem of ensuring continuity in the management of the process. What happens before the contract is signed has an influence on what happens afterwards. The alchemical reaction in Paint Inc. provides a double illustration of this phenomenon. First of all, accepting to have special clauses that favour one company's employees is sowing the seeds of future difficulties with the other company's staff. Paint Inc. did not anticipate these problems. Then, the value of the companies and the price negotiated are likely to fluctuate after the first contacts have been established. When Michael Edertour squeezed Bernard Bloq's fingers, the latter decided "to make him pay dearly", all the more so as he knew that he held the upper hand in the negotiations. By buying Core Paint for a high price, Michael Edertour was obliged to review his plans for creating the value hoped for, thus increasing the risk of difficulties later on. In the end, the phase of achievements was not well prepared.

In brief, the way that the phase of hopes is conducted has repercussions on the outcome of the acquisitions. Right from the preliminary stages, it is in the buyer's best interests to prepare the implementation of the merger. That is why the appointment of a pilot is absolutely necessary: thanks to his overall view of the financial, strategic and organizational elements of the operation, he is able to design the chief orientations of the integration plan and, if necessary, act before the contract is signed in order to create conditions that will favour integration of the companies.

Choosing the pilot of hopes

The pilot during the phase of hopes therefore leads a team of specialists. Three objectives can be set for him. First of all, provide his management with all the information and analyses that will enable them to decide whether or not to acquire the target company. Second, prepare an integration plan that will enable the strategic plan to materialize. Third, launch if necessary the phase of achievements (i.e., the actions that are supposed to make the actual merger easier).

This task can fall to the managing director when the buyer is a small- or medium-size company. In a big group, the technical nature of the analyses often means that a mergers and acquisitions specialist is selected. Thanks to his experience in transactions, such a pilot has usually acquired diverse skills in finance, law, strategy and negotiations and knows how to articulate these competencies. This expertise helps him to construct an overall picture of the project. Thanks to the networks he has developed both inside and outside the company, he is able to quickly assemble a competent team, made up of employees and external consultants.

One alternative, although not used very often, is to appoint the director of a business unit or of a profit centre. The range of his managerial experience guarantees his ability to arrange and manage the strategic, financial, organizational and human elements involved. The choice of such a manager to the detriment of "an acquisitions' specialist" offers one advantage: since he is a manager in the line of business in which the target company operates, he will be in charge of integrating the target. The continuity of the process is thus ensured: the man who will be managing the phase of achievements will have specialized knowledge of the dossier and will have had previous contacts with the target. The learning process is already over, which makes a priori the implementation of the merger easier.

On the other hand, the profit centre manager can suffer from three weaknesses. He may be handicapped from the start when he tries to assemble his team, if he does not have a lot of personal contacts on the outside and if his position in the hierarchy prevents him from quickly mobilizing experts from different parts of his company. Second, he will find it difficult to manage current operations in his business unit and monitor the acquisition process at the same time. But, above all, several of the stories related in this book, including "The gold nugget" (Section 3.1), point to the very heavy workload that the people involved in every phase of the process have to undertake. If the same person oversees the whole of the process, there is the risk that he or she will end up totally exhausted.

That is why a compromise solution, used by experienced buyers, consists in having the first phase managed by a mergers and acquisitions specialist, incorporating into his team those people who will manage the integration process. The choice of pilot is crucial, but so is the selection of the members of his team.

The pilots of the achievements

Once he has taken over control, the buyer faces a double task: not only must he implement the changes planned, but he must also ensure the continued efficiency of ongoing business. Yet, this second mission is sometimes forgotten about. Csiszar and Schweiger (1994) explained the two factors necessary for the project to succeed: the generation of the expected additional value and the preservation of the companies' current values. The first factor concerns the effects of combining both partners; the second is concerned with the day-to-day management of each company individually: this now becomes a temporary activity and ceases when the reorganization has been completed and when the new organization is ready to function. So, the transition has to be managed and the changes introduced simultaneously. Since there are two objectives, preservation and value creation, two managers can be appointed. In reality, there is sometimes only one. When there are two of them, they have to work together to coordinate the actions aimed at preservation and those aimed at creating extra value. Figure 3.1 illustrates the need for project leaders throughout the process.

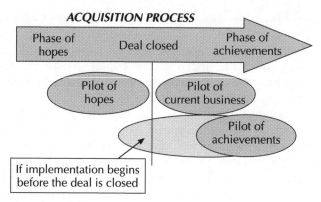

Figure 3.1   The pilots of the process.

Whatever solution is adopted, the pilot or pilots need to be carefully selected, for the stakes are high. These pilots are usually employees of the buyer or from the company taken over. The choice depends on a number of parameters: the strategic objective, the nature and size of the synergies, the price paid, a friendly or a hostile bid, how they plan to integrate both companies, knowledge of the business and the country of the company that has been acquired, assessment of the potential of the old management team, human resources available in-house, ... It is impossible to draw up an exhaustive list. In brief, the selection is closely linked to the context of the operation, to how the process unfolds during the phase of hopes and to the managers available.

In a study (Very and Schweiger, 2001) with David Schweiger, an American colleague, we discovered that buyers relied heavily on the executives of the company being bought when the transaction meant that they were entering a new country. Because they did not have any operations in this place, the buyers did not know a lot about the country, the customers, the products or the competition. That being the case, they usually relied on the target company's executives who did possess this knowledge. So, it is not surprising that certain responses to our survey pointed out that a lack of trust in the old management team constituted a deal-killer of paramount importance. Without trust there can be no acquisition.

In another study carried out with Stephen Gates (Gates and Very, 2001) we suggested that the choice of pilot for the integration was paramount. When the integration was entrusted to the financial director, the latter tended to use financial criteria in monitoring the progress of the process. When the integration was led by a business unit manager or a team leader, they tended to include non-financial criteria when monitoring progress of the process (employee satisfaction, retention of employees and customers, speed of integration, ...).

A team for realizing achievements

No team can make a bad deal good, but a bad team can make a good deal bad.

(Aiello and Watkins, 2000, p. 103)

Combining two companies is more or less complicated, according to the nature and the size of the changes to be brought about. The most complex cases are those that require a lot of reorganization, involving intense interrelationships and bringing together employees from two different companies. In brief, combining the two companies results in the creation of one single, new organization.[2] In these situations, the preparation and implementation of changes require teams, with each one working away at a particular objective, and the whole show being coordinated by the pilot of achievements. One team works on the exploitation of a synergy, the second designs the new hierarchical structure, the third deals with interfaces between information systems, the fourth looks for solutions to the problems of harmonizing human resources policies, the fifth works out a new strategy for a business unit, the sixth plans and manages the communications policy, ... The coordinator's role is therefore essential, because the work of some teams will have repercussions on other teams. The pilot's other major task consists in selecting the people who will make up these teams. When it comes to merging two computer systems, often a very tricky problem, the team sometimes needs external consultants, plus people who come from both companies and who are experts on their own systems. People from the company that has been acquired have to be identified and selected. This selection will be based on several criteria: competence, leadership and enthusiasm for the acquisition.[3] It is indeed unwise to recruit incompetent people, or those incapable of carrying along others with them, or even those who are not in favour of the new strategic plan. When the companies are of equal size, a requirement stipulating equality in numbers is sometimes added: the teams have to include the same number of people from each company. Some experienced buyers start this selection process during the due

---

[2] Integration in these cases is comparable with absorption or symbiosis, concepts described by Haspeslagh and Jemison (1991). The interested reader will find details on integration typology in Chapter 7.

[3] A fourth dimension will be considered later: the level of vigilance. It will be dealt with in Chapters 5 and 6.

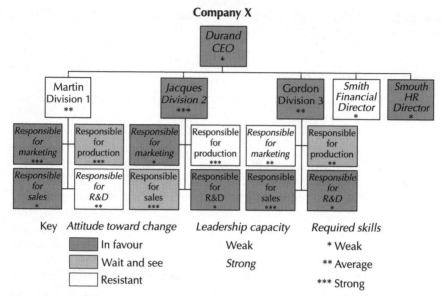

Figure 3.2   Identification of individual potential.

diligence investigations prior to the final negotiations. Figure 3.2 illustrates the type of representation used to carry out this selection. The buyer thus gains time by starting to form his teams before the deal has been closed.

In projects that are going to bring about a lot of change, we should point out that overhauling an organization requires the same type of work. The team in charge of designing the new structure is also in charge of putting forward names for each post in the hierarchy. This team will use similar criteria: skills for the function, motivation, leadership and possibly the need to ensure equity in terms of each firm's representation in top management posts. The story entitled "Fateful encounters" (Section 5.1 on p. 89) deals with the question of appointments. It will enrich the reader's imagination by adding a political dimension to the choice of people.

How the pilots work

When Lucent Technologies acquired Ascend Communications in 1999, an integration manager was appointed before the deal was closed. He immediately made up four teams that included people from each company. These teams used appropriate project management methods and tools to carry out their tasks. They each worked on one key issue: the customers, products, human resources and administration. Simulation exercises were carried out as early as April, whereas, the takeover did not take effect until June. The day the integration phase started, they were ready to make some reorganizations. The teams continued their work until October 1999 (Ashkenas and Francis, 2000).

It is worth noting that both the pilot of hopes and the pilot of achievements frequently use project management methods today. As a project is by its nature both unique and temporary, the person in charge of the transition is not concerned since he is managing ongoing business. The attempt to buy a target company is considered to be a project that is itself made up of numerous sub-projects in fields such as financial assessment, strategic valuation, law and taxation, ... With the help of appropriate methods, the pilot of hopes coordinates and integrates the results obtained by his teams into an overall picture, recruits people at the right moment, manages the time, the quality and the cost of his acquisition project. In a similar manner, the pilot of achievements leads his teams and coordinates the sub-projects that are devoted to the changes. Since a buyer cannot anticipate everything, each team has to adapt its initial plans when new findings emerge, find the most appropriate resources, deploy them and monitor the effectiveness of the transformations. The final objective is to achieve the strategic objectives and to create the value, in the volume and within the time limits set at the beginning. When the initial projections have been achieved, when the changes have been put into place, the project comes to an end and the company then enters a period of normal business management.

We will not go into any more detail about project management methods, because they have already been described in numerous works. On the other hand, to use them effectively, the buyer has to get organized in advance.

Preparing the organization for change

An opportunity does not wait: when it presents itself, the interested buyer has to be able to seize it. Otherwise, the seller will go and knock on other doors. That is why a strategy of development through acquisitions needs an organization that is ready to seize opportunities. For that, it is necessary to mobilize people quickly. So, the role of top management consists in designing an organization and outlining procedures that will make it easy to react and to have people at their disposal.

The construction of an organization that is conducive to acquisitions does not stop here. It also has to take into account how future acquisitions will be accommodated. The research carried out with David Schweiger (Very and Schweiger, 2001) produced several responses on this subject:

one company would move the management of a business unit to a foreign country considered to be particularly attractive in order to facilitate acquisitions there; another would assign to each business unit management team an acquisitions controller whose mission was to facilitate the integration of companies they had acquired.

Another organizational or formal problem concerns what happens when people return to their normal jobs. The return of people working on the integration to their initial posts has to be planned. Some of them will have been seconded full time to the project. They will wonder about their futures if nothing has been planned to manage their return to their old posts. In this type of situation the repercussions can be disastrous: people will not want to commit themselves to these strategic projects in the future.

So, this is one of the roles the human resources department takes on: planning the postings of team members at the end of their missions. Its other roles consist in:

- Spotting those employees with potential.
- Training them, either for project management, or to take up other responsibilities (project leader, managing the transition phase).
- Monitoring these members of staff: as the workload on such a project is usually greater than the average workload in the company, there is a risk that the people involved will be worn out morally and physically if they overdo it on this kind of mission.

Summary

The choice of pilots and team members is a tricky task, but one that is essential for the success of the acquisition project. The sooner the people are chosen, the quicker changes can be put in place. When, in addition, the buyer is ready to seize opportunities and to accommodate the targets, he facilitates the conduct of the acquisition process from the first analyses right up to the final integration.

Just like the tortoise we should set off at the right moment and proceed at a steady pace instead of dashing off too late like the hare and consequently wearing out our colleagues.

Chapter 4

Major M&A issues

4.1. STORY: THE CHRISTMAS PRESENT

The distribution of veterinary products requires a large investment in order to follow the growth of the market and establish a solid competitive position in the face of aggressive competitors. That was why V.E.L. had decided to concentrate its future investments in this sector. As its resources were limited, it had had to make choices. With the board's agreement, it had decided to dispose of the Q.V.E.L. division, which had only become a subsidiary one year beforehand. This division was in charge of distributing animal feed. It had been losing money for three years.

Dominik Piotch, the financial director, had been put in charge of the disposal. The subsidiary would be sold to the highest bidder. Dominik had held a meeting with his investment banker to discuss the open bid. They had agreed on the details of the banker's mission, had drawn up a schedule and had negotiated the banker's fee and how he would be paid. The banker would receive an initial sum of money for finding potential buyers, and then he would receive a "success fee". In other words, the banker would receive part of his fee only if the sale went through. The two men had written together the "blind teaser", a brief, anonymous description of Q.V.E.L. This two-page document contained information about the industry, the size of the subsidiary, as well as information about the main figures from the balance sheet and the profit and loss account. On the 9th November, the banker sent this document to about 60 companies in various countries, all of which were involved in the distribution of animal feed.

Replies flooded in right up to the 2nd December deadline. About 15 companies had shown an interest. In exchange for their signature on a confidentiality agreement, the banker sent them the "selling memorandum" that had been drawn up with V.E.L.'s senior management during the month of November. This 20-page dossier revealed to the potential buyers that the company for sale was a subsidiary of the V.E.L. group. The memorandum specified that it was a wholly owned subsidiary of V.E.L. The product ranges, the customer base and the competition were described; there was a presentation of the financial, human and technical resources. It gave a profile of the top management. The document began with a strategic diagnosis and ended with a financial analysis of the past and of the future. A timetable and a description of the different stages of the sale were attached to it.

In accordance with this timetable, the V.E.L. senior management received letters of interest from potential buyers two weeks later. Their impatience gave way to disappointment: the tenders were lower than they had hoped for. With the help of the investment bank, the V.E.L. senior management analysed each proposition meticulously. Some of them were eliminated because the price offered was judged to be ridiculously low. One tender from a direct competitor was immediately rejected for another reason: V.E.L. suspected that the competitor was merely seeking to obtain information for his own benefit. Despite the usual precautions and the agreements that had been signed, it was difficult to guard against such practices.

Then foreign companies were eliminated for reasons of price and the weak synergies that existed between them and Q.V.E.L. In fact, the world market in animal feed is not divided up evenly between countries. Each country or geographical region specializes in certain types of breeding: cattle, poultry, pigs, sheep ... Obviously the market in animal feed is organized according to the type of breeding each region of the planet specializes in. As Q.V.E.L. earned most of its turnover from cattle feed, they felt that there were few synergies that could be exploited with foreign distributors who dealt with other types of animal breeding. It would be better to merge with someone who specialized in cattle feed. Indeed, as far as the V.E.L. management was concerned, the greater the potential for synergies between Q.V.E.L. and the buyer, the higher the selling price would be.

After five days of analysis, discussions and reflection, four possible buyers were selected, either for their price proposition, or for their synergies potential. The initial disappointment was forgotten; on the 24th December, executives and bankers opened a bottle of champagne to celebrate the selection of the four bidders.

"That's one thing out of the way," said V.E.L.'s chairman, raising his glass of champagne. "Friends, we've just completed our list for Father Christmas; I hope he'll bring us one of the four presents we asked him for. One will be enough ... provided that he pays a lot of money!" They all burst out laughing. It was 5.00 p.m. when the phone rang.

Wox is looking for opportunities

On the 9th November, the day when V.E.L. set the sale in motion, Peter Kochet, development director of Wox Europe, had gathered together the ten members of his team in his office. The atmosphere was relaxed. Peter had just thanked the whole team, everyone from his secretary to his deputy. The team had worked hard during the previous two months, work that had produced a 50-page report outlining the development alternatives that could be envisaged in Europe over the next five years. The Wox Europe board of directors, and the board of the parent company in the USA, had appreciated the quality of the report and had congratulated Peter on behalf of his team. The Wox executives had decided to follow the report's recommendations: strengthen their competitive position in Europe in their main line of business, the manufacture of animal feed. Several target countries had been chosen. Development would come mainly through acquiring companies, depending on the acquisition opportunities that might arise. The majority of their investments would be dedicated to this type of growth over the next two years. Peter was happy. The Wox senior management trusted him, even though he had only been recruited the previous year. At the time, Wox had made considerable efforts to poach him from his consulting firm. Considering how things had turned out, he was now convinced that he had made the right choice. His team was assured of a key role in strategy from now on, for the board of directors had given him the responsibility of unearthing acquisition opportunities in the target countries. This is what Peter had just told his team. On that evening of the 9th November, the champagne flowed and some even spilled over onto Peter's office carpet.

The following weeks were devoted to finding working methods that would enable them to succeed in their new task. Peter had a lot of experience of acquisitions, gained through his previous job as a consultant. He redistributed some of the roles within his team, focusing several colleagues on the search for opportunities. An English financier, who specialized in the financial valuation of companies, joined the team. Peter also negotiated with his senior management the possibility of using experts from the Wox group to study potential targets. This type of secondment could involve experts in finance, human resources, R&D, communication or environmental protection. Business unit managers might also be needed. These secondments would occur according to need and for a set period of time. This method of working was approved and Wox Europe's staff and operations managers were informed.

Peter also contacted one of the biggest auditing and consulting firms in the world. This firm, like its fellow consultants, had opened a mergers and acquisitions department to take advantage of the large number of operations in this sector. Peter had read in the papers that this firm was well positioned in the market for advice on mergers and acquisitions, and had particular expertise in the food-processing industry. He had a meeting with one of the partners. The two men defined the terms and the content of the mission that Peter wanted to entrust to them. The following week, the consultants launched Operation TSFW, "Target Screening For Wox", aiming to identify targets to acquire in five European countries. A first report on this search was planned for the week before Christmas.

As agreed, the consultant presented his report on the 20th December. The prospects looked disappointing. In fact, in the countries targeted, the competition was oligopolistic with few competitors corresponding, at first sight, to Peter's criteria or who were likely acquisition targets. The two men had a long discussion about two companies whom they thought should be studied, although neither one was up for sale. Peter did not seem too happy with the prospects. The consultant then suggested that they should launch a second search, only this time they would be more flexible about the size and the profitability demanded of the target companies. Peter was sceptical. He promised to think about it.

On the morning of the 24th December, the consultant phoned Peter. He was keen to preserve his relationship with Peter and he had a good reason for calling. He informed him there was a company for sale in the feed distribution sector. Peter knew the V.E.L. group, which got some of its supplies from Wox. V.E.L. was well known in the distribution sector. The consultant argued that this target corresponded to their criteria concerning size, although it was positioned further down the line in the animal feed industry. He managed to persuade Peter to contact the seller. There would be no harm in enquiring. That same day, at 5.00 p.m., Peter picked up his phone and dialled the number the consultant had given him.

The new candidate

Dominik Piotch was still out of breath when he entered the CEO's office. After the celebrations, he had received the phone call that had caused him to run to his boss's office.

"We have a new candidate! You'll never guess who!"

Dominik then told him about his conversation with Peter Kochet. They had never studied the idea of a supplier as a potential buyer and the call from Wox had created turmoil in his mind. A powerful supplier, what could be better? There were bound to be strong synergies in such a merger, by economizing on transaction costs within the industry. These synergies would justify a high selling price. That was why Dominik had promised Peter Kochet a quick response concerning Wox's participation in the open bid.

The V.E.L. CEO also had the same intuition. Integrating a manufacturer into distribution was bound to increase his profitability.

"Dominik, we might have an opportunity here to get a price higher than the one we hoped for when we made our first selection of candidates. Listen, I'm going to cancel my Christmas holidays. Do the same. We'll meet on the 26th at 9.00 a.m. to see how we're going to integrate Wox into the process. I'll invite our banker to the meeting."

Dominik was delighted. He now had his excuse to cancel his week's holiday and he could thus avoid having to spend the week with his family in the French Périgord. Avoiding the traditional, gargantuan family meals would be good for his diet. He would make do with the fennel roots the nutritionist had recommended. He did not really like them, but he could see the effect they had on his weight: he had already lost five kilos. He now felt much better when he played his usual Friday evening game of football with his friends. And, besides, this was the only real moment of relaxation he gave himself outside his work.

As for Peter, he had been impressed by the instant enthusiasm shown by Dominik Piotch on the phone. Reacting promptly to his request for information, the selling company's financial director had spoken highly of the advantages of such an acquisition. He had explained that V.E.L. had only prospected among competitors to find a buyer. The possibility of Q.V.E.L. being acquired by a supplier looked interesting at first sight. Dominik would inform his management of Peter's interest. He promised him a quick reply.

Events seemed to be going too quickly for Peter. He had phoned just to make an enquiry and now he found himself already in the position of possible buyer. "Let's keep a cool head," he said to himself. "It's true that there aren't many acquisition opportunities that correspond to the orientations we have fixed for ourselves. However, if we acquired Q.V.E.L., it would not be in line with our strategic thinking. We haven't studied this option. Should we charge in or drop out?"

Father Christmas visited Peter's house as planned on the evening of the 24th. The next morning, while his children were excitedly opening their presents, Peter was still thinking about Q.V.E.L. All day long he weighed up the advantages and disadvantages and had difficulty sleeping that night. By Monday morning he had decided. They would have to analyse this acquisition opportunity. Although it was not in line with the route they had chosen for Wox's development, studying the opportunity presented at least two interests: testing the strategy of acquiring operations further down their line of business, an option they had not initially considered at Wox; and testing the organization he had set up with his team for acquiring companies.

The meeting on the 26th December at V.E.L. officially confirmed Wox as the fifth candidate selected for negotiations. Peter was informed immediately by phone and he responded favourably. He sent his approval by courier, along with a confidentiality agreement. The following day he received by fax a document that outlined the next stages of the procedure. Two days later, he received the "selling memorandum".

Wox gets organized

Peter was still suffering from the New Year celebrations. When he walked into his office on the 2nd January, in his sober, grey suit, he smiled as he thought about his colleagues: they would not suspect in the least that he had spent the evening singing his head off to karaoke videos. He was wrong: his secretary quickly spotted the huge dark rings under his eyes, a sure sign of his hangover. She also noted the hoarseness in his vocal cords and the tremor in his voice whenever he wished someone a happy New Year. Some of his colleagues even asked him if he was ill. In fact, everyone realized that he was suffering from a terrible hangover. After two cups of very strong coffee, Peter immersed himself in the V.E.L. dossier. Along with his consultant, he had devoted the last few days of the month of December to making a preliminary study of the target company. Then they had thought about how to make up the team. They would need various specialists to complement their own fields of expertise. Peter had phoned or left messages with six staff managers in Wox. He expected their replies by the 2nd January.

Peter then had a meeting with those departmental colleagues who would be involved in the dossier. He explained the acquisition opportunity and requested their absolute discretion. He also explained how the team would work, described the procedure for the sale drawn up by V.E.L. and pointed out that six in-house experts would be joining them at different stages of the project.

When he was back in his office, he made enquiries about the experts he had requested. Of the six managers he had contacted, only one had replied and had agreed to second one of his management team. Peter had no news from the other five. He had to contact them again, present them with his arguments and even threaten to hire experts from outside Wox, in order to convince them. Reluctantly, they all finally agreed to send one of their people. Although they had initially been favourable to the idea, they now saw in practice that seconding a person, even if it was only for two or three days, disrupted the running of their departments.

Peter spent most of the next two days planning the work. He carefully reread the V.E.L. document that explained the procedure they had chosen for the sale of their subsidiary. Then he identified the tasks to be accomplished and he arranged them in order, using his experience to guide him. He planned when he would call on the six in-house experts. He also outlined the role the consultants would play in the project. Once the resources had been planned and allocated to tasks, he worked out a schedule and got down to estimating costs. After that, he budgeted the operation before integrating all the different elements into an action plan. It was only a crude outline that would need to be adapted, but it would help them to conduct the study of the target company.

While Peter was busy creating his team and planning the action, his colleagues were gathering up a maximum of information about V.E.L., Q.V.E.L. and the animal feed distribution market from outside sources. It was a very competitive market and was more or less mature, depending on the segments and the types of animals. Q.V.E.L. had a large market share in the cattle feed segment. However, faced with more aggressive and innovative competitors, its position had started to erode these last few years. This deterioration was accompanied by a financial performance that was lower than the average for this line of business. Efforts had been made recently to improve internal efficiency and the quality of their customer services. These improvements were expected to bear fruit in six months' time, leading to a reconquest of their markets.

At first sight, the balance sheet looked healthy and the subsidiary did not seem to need a massive injection of financial resources. In brief, Q.V.E.L. appeared to be a leader who had rested on its laurels and who was now looking for its second wind.

Q.V.E.L. had two main suppliers: Wox and one of its direct competitors. In acquiring Q.V.E.L., Wox would have access, not only to a reputed
know-how, but also to customers. This direct contact with the customer base, particularly powerful breeders groups, could prove to be a decisive advantage in the future: Wox would have a much better idea of customer needs and would thus be able to innovate with more precision. Peter could foresee some very promising synergies if the two companies merged.

At the end of the first week, the team made a summary of the information they had gathered and drew up the next few days' investigation plan. This plan concerned either areas in which very little information had been collected, or areas where the information was judged not to be reliable. The team agreed on the tools they would use for analysis and the sources of data they would examine. The work was divided up among the team members. Peter also updated his schedule.

The following Monday, two nice surprises landed on his desk. First of all, he received from the USA the in-house documentation relating to the acquisition procedure. Based on past acquisitions, the manual explained the internal procedure that had to be followed in acquiring a target company. At different stages of the process, Peter would have to seek his management's approval to continue studying and negotiating. The document also contained a checklist of the points to be investigated during the acquisition process. Finally, about ten deal-killers (i.e., criteria that have to be satisfied in order for negotiations to be pursued) were listed: if the acquisition did not satisfy one of these deal-killers, the operation had to stop immediately. Peter noticed that most of the deal-killers concerned fraudulent or unethical practices.

The other good news came via the Wox intranet. A message from the USA informed Peter that he now had access to DABAXA, the Wox database on acquisitions. "At last!" Peter sighed. He had made his request a week ago. The group had just created DABAXA and he was one of its first users. He accessed the database using the procedure laid down. It contained a myriad of information about 30 acquisitions the group had made during the last 12 years. Peter could do a sort by industry, by country, by size of company or by any other variable. For every acquisition listed, he had the details of the person in charge and of the team members who had taken part. Peter had carte blanche to contact any of them if he wanted to. DABAXA was linked to another database called DABAXAR, which contained, for every acquisition, all the documents that had been produced and exchanged with the seller or outside contributors. DABAXAR was itself linked to DABOX, a database that supplied a set of blank documents that the team studying the target company could use: examples of letters of intent, examples of contracts with consultants and bankers, ... Along with these examples there were grids for accountancy analyses, for strategic or financial valuations, all of them programmed to be used on a spreadsheet.

"Woh! This is brilliant!" Peter exclaimed. As soon as he had some free time, he immersed himself in DABAXA. Unfortunately, after two hours spent sorting and studying cases, he noted that none of them corresponded to the Q.V.E.L. context. There were no cases of integration with a company that operated further down the food products distribution chain. Peter was disappointed. Nevertheless, his search had not been in vain. One of the recent acquisitions in the USA concerned a service company, of similar size to Q.V.E.L., which had also been losing momentum. He drew some interesting lessons from it concerning key points to be studied and he was able to identify an American who specialized in the service sector. This person was a member of the Wox group who had taken part in the whole acquisition process from the first contacts with the target company right up to the integration. After the acquisition, he had been seconded for a year to the new management team of the company that had been acquired. Peter decided to phone this person to discuss the Q.V.E.L. project. If this man could bring some added value to the project, Peter would try to get hold of his services.

Peter then printed off a set of blank documents and gave them out to his team according to their needs. He also downloaded for his colleagues the program used for financial valuations. The database had been useful after all.

The Q.V.E.L. valuation

Meanwhile, V.E.L.'s banker had organized the next stages in the procedure. Rooms in a luxury hotel had been booked in which to set up the "data-room". Each potential buyer would have his turn in this room. He would be allowed 48 hours to consult a set of documents that Dominik and his banker had jointly selected. The potential buyers would have access to the company's statutes, to various contracts, to the portfolio of customers, to some elements of their cost structure, to the accounting methods used, ... Q.V.E.L. apparently had nothing to hide.

When it was Wox's turn, Peter went to the hotel with the members of his team. Two experts from the Wox group joined them for the 48 hours: a lawyer and the American service industry specialist, who had impressed Peter on the phone. Each person had a specific investigation to carry out and worked hard to complete it in the time allowed. The V.E.L. banker saw to it that everything ran smoothly. The documents that had been supplied were fairly complete, underlining V.E.L.'s desire to go through with the sale. The Wox team began to get a more precise picture of Q.V.E.L.

Afterwards, the seller invited each potential buyer in turn to the subsidiary's head office. They were able to meet the senior management, to assess the working atmosphere and to learn something of the internal organization. Peter had added a new person to his team: a headhunter. He worked in tandem with the in-house human resources expert. Together both of them conducted in-depth interviews with the top executives of the subsidiary. The objective was to test their motivation and to assess their competence.

It was now time to make a first synthesis. The whole team met for one afternoon: the people from Wox Europe and the consultants were present in the room; the American contributors took part by videoconference. The information was shared and discussed. Three subjects were tackled in succession: the valuation of Q.V.E.L. and the synergies, areas of doubt that remained and the preparation of an integration plan if the sale went through.

The first impressions concerning the strategic positioning and the financial health of the target company were confirmed. Q.V.E.L. was losing momentum, but had taken measures to put that right in the near future. In addition, those who had been in the data-room had noted the low level of investment these last few years. It was obvious that Q.V.E.L.

had not been a priority for V.E.L. for a long time. This could explain the deterioration in its performance. Another weak point had been identified: the management of supplies and stocks left something to be desired. As this weakness stood out clearly in the documents supplied, Peter wondered if it had not been deliberately highlighted. In fact, it is fairly easy to modify a stocks management policy. And Peter knew that some sellers did highlight minor deficiencies in order to hide more serious problems. In so doing, the seller hopes to attract and focus the buyer's attention on a minor detail. In this game of cat and mouse, Peter had no intention of ending up the loser. That was why the discussion quickly moved on from the stocks management problem.

At this stage of the analysis, the results of the investigations were translated into figures and then integrated into the models used for valuing the target company and the synergies. Different hypotheses were worked out as to how quickly Q.V.E.L. could be put back onto its feet. The strong competitive environment was taken into account in the simulation exercises, by examining the sensitivity of profits to a price reduction. Then the valuation was put to one side for a while.

The discussion moved on to areas of doubt that still persisted. The VEL management had supplied very little information on their human resources management policy. The American service industry specialist advised them to ask for more information. Then, it was time to study how customers might react. In fact, by entering the distribution market, Wox would become a competitor to its other customers. How would they react to this announcement? Would they change supplier? A sub-project team was set up to study these questions.

Peter then presented the main lines of the future integration plan. Barely had he started speaking when a colleague pointed out the big cultural differences that existed between both companies. The "distribution" culture seemed far removed from the "production culture".

"These differences don't matter. We're not thinking of merging both companies since they do different jobs. My plan is for Q.V.E.L. to have a large measure of autonomy in its operations. We'll focus the merger on two axes: a rapid exploitation of synergies and a progressive evolution of organizational structures."

The synergies affected Wox's production department: it was expecting to achieve economies of scale in manufacturing, as the volume of sales would increase considerably. These synergies and the cost of implementing them were calculated. In six months' time it expected to have achieved some gains. The progressive evolution of Q.V.E.L.'s structure was a tricky subject. Whereas Wox was organized along six hierarchical levels, Q.V.E.L. only had four. Employees' status and the breakdown of responsibilities had been modified in Q.V.E.L. during the last year. Peter feared a fierce reaction to any new changes. That was why he was proposing a gentle, progressive evolution. His other argument centred on the fact that the different nature of the businesses meant that they had to adapt to the characteristics of each one. In fact, harmonization was not urgent. The human resources department would study ways of going about it after Q.V.E.L. had been acquired. Everyone in the team agreed. Just as they did for the synergies, they worked out a schedule and a preliminary estimation of the costs. The economies of scale, the investments and the expenditure were then integrated into the financial valuation of the project. Peter was fairly pleased with the result: the acquisition could a priori be paid for in cash. In terms of financing it, there would be no problems.

"There remains one point to be resolved," Peter said. "Who will manage Q.V.E.L.?"

It was 9.00 p.m. Worn out, some members of the team asked for the question to be discussed the following day. However, Peter insisted on an immediate response.

"We have to decide quickly. It's crucial! In fact, we don't know the distribution business very well. Yet we need to have an experienced team at the head of Q.V.E.L. Should we continue with the existing team, especially when we have doubts about the CEO's competence and the sales director's motivation? Sorry, but we have to decide now. If we need to recruit, it would be a good thing to act quickly for the deal will be closed in three or four weeks' time."

They knew that Peter was right, so they opened their dossiers again. They reached a decision around 10.00 p.m.: two new people would be recruited. Peter was satisfied. Replacing the CEO would be seen by the employees as a symbol of Wox's desire to breathe new life into the subsidiary and to make it profitable again. The moment was right for change.

On the road home, Peter was deep in thought. Despite the cold, he was driving with his window down so as not to fall asleep. He was exhausted. Piloting the acquisition process was a test of nerve. He wanted it to succeed, but he did not want to find any skeletons in the closet after the sale. His career depended on it. On the other hand, he was spending so much time at work that he only saw his children at the weekend. Fortunately, his wife was very understanding, but he could not go on for ever like this. This period of intense activity reminded him of his time as a consultant. And to think that he had changed jobs so that he could spend more time with his family!

Peter was also worried about his team. Although they were very loyal to him, they were also very tired and were bound to be neglecting their families as well. Peter would have to keep them motivated until the end of the process. Then, he would give them some time off.

"For the next target I'll choose other people," he said to himself. Then he came back to his first thoughts.

"What a poisoned chalice! Because of all this work I still haven't recovered from my New Year celebrations. Only my vocal cords have got better." A glance in the rear-view mirror confirmed his thoughts: two large dark circles under his eyes stared back at him. When he arrived home, he fell into his wife's arms. She kissed him and said: "Darling! We've been invited next Saturday to a karaoke evening at the Capellaci's. I accepted straight away. It'll be a change for you, it'll do you good."

The decision

The following Monday, Peter arrived two hours late for work, sloppy and dishevelled. His shirt tail was hanging out, one end of his shirt collar was sticking up and his tie was hanging loosely around his neck. His secretary looked at him in astonishment.

"Are you not well, Mr Kochet?"

Peter walked up to her and whispered in her ear: "I've lost my voice. I can't speak. Come into my office and we'll deal with urgent matters now, and then I want to be left in peace all morning. Ah! I'm forgetting the most important thing: bring me two cups of strong coffee, please."

The morning was hard, very hard. Whenever he came out of his office, at least one colleague would jokingly try to imitate Joe Cocker's gritty version of *With A Little Help From My Friends*, with a slight smile on his face. How difficult it was to hide his hangover! Peter started to become more productive during the afternoon. He worked with the team's two financial experts, and they updated their valuation of Q.V.E.L. using the results of the latest investigations. Then they discussed the price they would offer. The Wox group had defined its own criteria concerning returns on investment. The three men decided on a price range that took account of these criteria, using several different methods as the in-house acquisitions manual demanded. And, no matter what hypothesis was used in their simulation exercises, they would still have a return on their investment in Q.V.E.L. in three years' time if the price paid stayed within this range. Peter took comfort from this result. He spent the next two days summarizing the analyses and putting it all into a 40-page report. Then, in accordance with Wox's internal procedure, it was time to get the opinion of the European board of directors.

Meanwhile, Dominik Piotch was very worried. All the potential buyers had expressed the same wish: to have more information about their human resources before they would declare their bids. Dominik took his banker to task:

"I told you it wouldn't work. These people weren't born yesterday. Besides none of them have spoken to us about supplies and stocks management. What are we going to do now?"

"Listen, we tried and it didn't work. It's not so serious. Your objective is to get rid of Q.V.E.L. We'll manage it, but no doubt for a lower price than we had envisaged."

"Good grief! Just remember that the first bids weren't exactly mouthwatering! Now what are we going to get? Pennies!"

"Oh, stop despairing. My advice is to be open with the buyers. Let them have a lot of information about the human resources. As for us, we'll review our valuations and our prices."

"Ah, if only we had had time to prepare the subsidiary for the sale . . ." Dominik thought.

Following this conversation, both men organized new meetings with each of the bidders and showered them with information. The people sent by Peter identified several problems: too many administrative staff, differences in salaries with Wox for administrative posts and a very restrictive agreement between employees and the company. When Peter heard the news, he called a meeting to assess the importance of these difficulties and to determine how to eliminate them. In the end they came to the conclusion that, since Q.V.E.L. would be run autonomously, these problems were minor ones. They would be resolved in due course. Nevertheless, all this would enable them to negotiate a lower price. Peter pointed out that these difficulties would pose more problems for the other potential buyers, who must be counting on merging teams. They would have to bear this fact in mind during the negotiations. For the tenth time, Peter reviewed the projections and the costs linked to the acquisition and recalculated his acceptable price range.

Wox Europe's board of directors met on the last Monday of January. Each member of the board had received the most recent version of the dossier that Peter's team had created. Using the information supplied, the objective of the meeting was to answer two questions: Should we negotiate to acquire Q.V.E.L.? If yes, were the price range and the proposed methods of financing acceptable?

The board discussed the first point only. Their discussion lasted more than three hours. Two directors insulted each other. Coffee was spilled on the carpet. A vase was broken. After three hours there was a majority decision. Of course, they would all stick together when the decision was applied.

The managing director of the European subsidiary sent for Peter:

"Mr Kochet, Wox won't be buying Q.V.E.L."

Peter felt as if he had been hit on the head with a hammer. "Wox won't be buying Q.V.E.L.? That's impossible," he thought. His mind wandered for a moment, and then he concentrated again on what he was being told.

"I won't hide from you that it was a difficult decision to take. However, acquiring Q.V.E.L. would mean having to question the strategic choices we made two months ago. Remember: you were the initiator. We must stick to our orientations in the next few months. To alter our strategy you would have to prove that it wasn't the right one or that it was too difficult to implement."

Peter nodded in agreement. They would make a bid that would be too low to interest the seller. Back in his office Peter chewed over the decision. It was true that he had forgotten the group's strategic objectives, so involved had he been in the acquisition project. Perhaps he should have submitted the project to the board earlier, although the procedure made no mention of such a step. However, it was not the right time for lamentations. He called an extraordinary meeting of his team and he prepared what he would say. Announcing the news to them would not be easy. They had sweated blood and tears to bring their mission to a successful conclusion. In the end, all their work was going to be of no avail. He decided he would finish on a positive note. Other identical cases would come up in the future. What's more, the project might have continued, but without any guarantee of success: another buyer might have won. And then the team had every reason to be proud of itself: they had worked well together and a lot of useful lessons could be drawn from this adventure. There would be a meeting in the near future to take stock of what they had achieved.

While waiting for his colleagues to arrive, he picked up the phone and dialled his wife's number:

"Hello darling! How are you? Could you organize a karaoke evening for this weekend? I feel like letting my hair down!"

On the 7th February, the date that had been fixed for final bids, Dominik Piotch received Wox's proposition. He had been eagerly awaiting it. In fact, the disclosure of the information about the human resources management had led the main bidders to offer very unattractive prices. As Dominik feared, these bidders must have felt that it would be very difficult to merge the sales teams and the administrative posts. That was why he was betting on the Wox solution, which would be based on a vertical integration. He tore open the envelope and read the proposition. It left him mouth open and his face rigid. He could not understand it.

"I'm fed up, totally fed up! All that effort for almost nothing! Selling this subsidiary is a poisoned chalice. Whatever possessed me to accept? Talk of a Christmas present!"

He would ask Peter for an explanation. Obviously, that would not change anything. Now, he had to organize the next stages in the procedure: pass on the bids to the V.E.L. board, select the candidate for the last round, negotiate the agreement and get a signature on the letter of intent, before starting the final negotiations, all of which would keep him under pressure for at least another two weeks.

"What a marathon!" he sighed, sitting there with both hands on his stomach. "What's more, the sale of Q.V.E.L. has caused me to miss the last two games of football. Still, looking on the positive side, I've lost four kilos in a month thanks to this project and the fennel roots. Here, that gives me an idea."

He called his Friday evening teammates and told them about his idea. They all agreed enthusiastically, so he asked his secretary to come in:

"Assia, would you please book a table for 15 people at the l'Auberge du Canard Gavé[1] for this Friday at 10.00 p.m.?"

"But, Dominik, this restaurant specializes in duck confit! What about your diet?"

"The price of duck has gone down. I'm taking advantage of that to give up my diet ..." he answered evasively, already thinking about the post-match celebrations on Friday.

For, after all, life wasn't only about work. "The price of friendship is worth more than the price of Q.V.E.L.," he thought.

4.2. STARS AND STORMS[2]

"The Christmas present" complements the story in Section 3.1, "The gold nugget". Both of them are concerned with the management of the phase of hopes. This story of the relationship between Wox and V.E.L. highlights several ideas and research findings that were presented in Chapter 3. However, there is one major difference between the two stories – the manner in which the acquisitions process was initiated: in spite of the fact that he follows identical steps, the buyer has little control over how the process unfolds when it is organized in the form of an auction by the seller; the buyer has to submit to the rhythm imposed on him, knowing that he is competing against other bidders. He is taking part in a game of cat and mouse organized from the start by a seller whispering to him: "You'll get the true facts ... if I sell!" There is no need to say anymore, the stories speak for themselves.

---

[1] Literally "the Inn of the Stuffed Duck".

[2] Translation of the magical title of a French book, *Etoiles et Tempêtes*, by Gaston Rébuffat, a famous mountaineer and writer on mountain climbing. Acquisition targets are gazed on like the stars, but sometimes they stir up storms ...

This section is devoted to the acquisition strategy and its implementation. First of all, we will reflect on the link between strategy and acquisition. Then we will discuss difficulties that arise, which are linked to the implementation of this strategy and the value creation project. Will the acquirer systematically encounter every one of the problems, as the literature seems to suggest?

But what has happened to my strategy?

Up to now, we have said that acquisitions had to fit into a clear strategic plan. The short story entitled "The Christmas present" shows that infatuation with and investment in an acquisition project sometimes make you lose sight of the strategic orientations chosen beforehand. When development through acquisitions is decided on, you can depict your ideal strategic target, the one that will enable you to achieve your objectives. Unfortunately, this often remains just a picture in your mind. Let's look at cases where the ideal does and does not exist.

The ideal exists, but is not for sale

In the case where the strategic ideal does exist, then it has to be acquired, and acquired properly. Not every shareholder, no matter what is said, is ready to part with his shares, even for an attractive price. Sentimental considerations come into play, like the importance of the name and the reputation in some family businesses. Certain executives who do not want to lose their place will fight tooth and nail to maintain the status quo. When ego gets involved ... if the main shareholders do not want to give in, the buyer will have to proceed in a hostile manner, or give up or wait for a more suitable moment to reiterate his offer. Pasteur Mérieux fought three years to acquire the Canadian vaccines company Connaught, as the target company was opposed to the takeover. For the senior management of Pasteur Mérieux, Connaught was at that time the ideal target to enable them to become world leader in what was already a market dominated by a few competitors. The merger was bound to be profitable thanks to the complementarity of the markets served and the creation of a critical mass in research and development. Once the deal was closed, the new group took more time than planned to exploit the R&D synergies, due to the unfriendly atmosphere that had pervaded the operation and the differences in R&D working methods.

The ideal exists and is for sale

Let's suppose that the owners agree to study the proposition. The buyer then finds himself in Michael Edertour's situation, the Paint Inc. CEO who wanted to take control of Core Paint. Poor management of the process, which led to the failure to anticipate the consequences of the contract they signed, created headaches for Edertour and his employees. The way the project is conducted can destroy the ideal situation.

On the other hand, a target selected for its ideal strategic positioning may harbour technological or huge organizational weaknesses. Since you cannot know everything in advance, your vision remains in part the fruit of your imagination or intuition and certain weaknesses may escape your notice. When, later on, you are living with your conquest, you will learn a lot more about her and you will discover that she has a way of doing things that does not necessarily correspond to what you were expecting. The investments and reorganization costs required will amount to a very large sum of money, which is likely to weaken the financial balance of your company. In addition, your takeover of the target company will be seen by its employees as a crucial event in their organization's history. There is the risk that your arrival, your actions or non-actions will provoke unfavourable reactions. If you are perceived as something negative, the operating mechanisms may break down once the acquisition has been made. A target is a tree whose foliage is all you can see at first. When you get closer, you uncover its internal structure, the trunk, the branches, a nest, and the ivy that is progressively strangling its growth. When you climb up the tree without taking precautions, you may end up shaking the boughs, knocking leaves off and causing the birds to fly away. Even worse, you could break a big branch, fall and crash to the ground. The tree might have suffered; you yourself are bruised and weakened. The moral: it is not because you have acquired a target that is a priori ideal for your chosen development strategy that you will achieve your strategic and financial objectives.

The ideal company does not exist

Now let's look at the situation where none of the targets identified corresponds exactly to your strategic ideal. This is what most frequently happens. Other targets are possible, but they do not really have the profile you are looking for. As your objective is to grow through acquisitions, you are going to select one or several companies that can be acquired. These targets are inserted into your long-term strategic vision – however, do check that they fit into this vision[3] – but they are

---

[3] I have deliberately not mentioned opportunities that lead to a radical alteration of a company's orientations. An example of this is the acquisition of Seagram by Vivendi. This swing from one type of business to another, a specific characteristic of some conglomerates, is relatively infrequent.

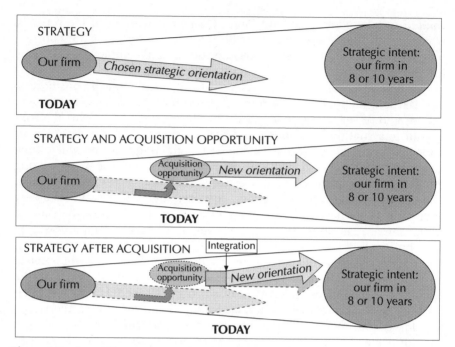

Figure 4.1   Acquisition and strategic orientation.

usually to be found at the edge of the route you have traced out for the next two or three years. Part of the business does not interest you, the complementarity of the countries served is not perfect, numerous duplicate posts exist, ... Thus, the acquisition of Zanussi by Electrolux in the 1980s corresponded to the ultimate objective of establishing European, then world leadership. Nevertheless, Electrolux had to adapt its strategy: a company that bought numerous components, it was now acquiring a company that manufactured them – a vertical integration. The result was the creation of the Electrolux Component Group within the structure of the new conglomerate (Ghoshal and Haspeslagh, 1990). The acquisition of a target that is not made to measure therefore takes the company down a path that is fairly distant from the one it had mapped out, as Figure 4.1 illustrates. You have to be aware of this and examine the consequences before deciding to acquire. This is what the members of Wox Europe's board of directors did in the story "The Christmas present". Their analysis of the dossier that Peter Kochet had put together persuaded them not to acquire Q.V.E.L., as this would drag the company in a direction that was too far from the strategic axes chosen a short time beforehand. For this reason it can be beneficial to call in deciders who were not involved when the process was under way. The latter are relatively neutral and can examine the project with a cool head. That is why many companies use deal-killers. Carefully drawn up – and not limited merely to ethical problems – these deal-killers are safeguards against the acquisition of any old target at any old price.

Let's suppose you have decided to acquire company X. You have chosen a new orientation related to the characteristics of your target: this direction represents the basis of the strategic plan that you want the employees of both companies to subscribe to. So, you become the owner of X and you combine the organizations. You now start to learn how the acquired company functions, thus gradually reducing the initial scarcity of information. You uncover weaknesses and strengths that were hidden. This new situation may lead you to not only adapt the integration methods, but also to partially modify the strategic plan. For example, the discovery of an R&D project lying dormant might encourage you to launch a new business activity, although this opportunity was not taken into account during the phase of hopes. Another situation that arises frequently – too frequently – is the impossibility of exploiting a synergy, which prompts you to lower the forecasts of expected cash flows. The bottom part of Figure 4.1 illustrates this potential influence on your strategy.

In brief, it is desirable – and logical – for the tactic of development through acquisitions to be part of the acquirer's strategic plan. However, the implementation of this manoeuvre may have an effect on the orientations chosen for the company. Acquiring can inject new blood into a firm's strategy.

Major difficulties during the phase of achievements

As just mentioned, the choice of target and the adaptation of the integration plan have consequences for companies' strategies and financial health, and therefore for the value creation project. That is why these consequences need to be anticipated as much as possible. To do this, acquirers frequently carry out due diligence investigations that aim to audit certain functions and practices of the target company and to identify eventual problems, hidden weaknesses or strengths. The results confirm or invalidate the valuations made during the phase of hopes. An extra audit is sometimes carried out in the weeks following the change of ownership, the conditions of the acquisition being subject to the conclusions of this investigation. To complement this due diligence investigation which is often focused on the intrinsic value of the target company, it is in the buyer's interest to think about the difficulties that might arise from the implementation of his integration plan. Let's discuss this latter point which often turns out to be crucial for the final success of the project.

In Section 1.2, I mentioned five difficulties that are commonly associated with failure. Paying too high a price usually results from poor management of the phase of hopes: the acquirer yields to pressures, emotions come into play, and, in the end, the price exceeds a reasonable sum. If paying an "irrational" additional premium then affects the integration, it is a cause of the problem and not strictly speaking an integration problem itself. A second difficulty, the discovery of "skeletons in the closet", can be defined as anything that could not have been anticipated during pre-acquisition investigations. We'll forget about it here. So, three problems remain that are likely to appear during the phase of achievements. These are individual reactions, collective reactions and external events. We are going to examine these difficulties in more detail, using academic research as the basis of our discussion. Subdividing these three categories of problem, researchers have underlined five major obstacles; they are presented below.

The voluntary departure of talented people

The talents of key employees are those that represent a large part of the value of one of the two companies, or that have a major role to play in the value creation process. In a family-owned company, where the managing director is the head of the family, his links with the main customers are usually based on a long, common history of trust and loyalty. If he leaves abruptly, so will the customers. In an electronics company, it could be the head of research and development, someone who created the innovative dynamism that has become an essential source of their competitiveness. In a boiler-making company, it could be a welder who possesses rare skills in welding techniques that enable the company to manufacture sophisticated equipment. This gives the company an advantage, as it is difficult for new competitors to break into this market if they do not possess similar skills. Whether they are top executives, middle management or simple employees, their departure jeopardizes the project. So, it is essential to handle these essential resources well. During initial negotiations measures are often taken to enlist their future services should the transaction be concluded (Very, 1999). Finally, we should not forget that the first people to resign are generally the best ones, because they will find it easier to get a new job.

Individual ambiguities and uncertainties

Even when he is not worried about his job being safe, the abrupt change of ownership raises questions for the employee concerning his career prospects, his salary and benefits, his working conditions, ... Each employee is living in a world of uncertainties and is waiting for answers. This period of questioning is frequently accompanied by a decrease in productivity. The buyer is therefore obliged to act immediately after the acquisition. This phase, called the "first 100 days", is important for displaying his leadership, rallying energies behind the common strategic plan and installing a climate that is conducive to the implementation of the project (Haspeslagh and Jemison, 1991). The buyer has to communicate a lot and keep people informed. Here, another danger lies waiting: the creation of ambiguities. According to Larsson and Risberg (1998), ambiguity arises in the individual when he hears contradictory information coming from different channels. This ambiguity disconcerts and creates distrust. Unlike uncertainty, which can be dispelled by clarifying things and giving out more information, it is much more complex to get rid of ambiguities. This requires reorganization of the channels and flow of communication to ensure harmonization of the information given out.

Power games and political tactics

Radical changes usually upset the balance of power, at least in the company that has been acquired. First of all, managers in high positions in the hierarchy frequently see an acquisition as a loss of "relative standing". Hambrick and Cannella (1993) studied this phenomenon: employees usually compare their status with that of counterparts who move in a similar social circle. When a company is acquired, the directors find themselves in a new environment and inevitably compare their new status with that of their counterparts in the other company as well as with the status they enjoyed before the acquisition. Most of them reach the conclusion that they have lost some standing: beforehand, they were big fish in a relatively small pond, now they have become small fish in a very big pond. This explanation has been put forward to help us understand why top executives leave voluntarily.

Reorganizations and reallocations can also result in political games. Whereas the majority see instability as a threat, other players might view it as an opportunity. They try to control certain areas of uncertainty. They manoeuvre to obtain, develop and use power and other rare resources which will then enable them to achieve their personal objectives: promotion, responsibility, remuneration, ... If the organization is not careful, it will become a hotbed of strife typified by the withholding of information, the creation of scapegoats, the manipulation or construction of underground, interpersonal networks (Pfeffer, 1980). Some of these tactics are exposed in the story "The Meletev cocktail" (Section 6.1 on

p. 115). If power games are part of life in a company and create a suboptimal way of working, it is obviously dangerous to let them develop too much.

Cultural resistance

Cultural resistance refers to the collective reaction displayed by the staff of a company to the loss of its identity and of the values and standards of behaviour that characterized the organization. This group of people is opposed to the implementation of the new strategic plan and thus threatens the success of the acquisition. We will examine more fully problems of a cultural nature in the next chapter because there are many inaccuracies surrounding this subject.

Loss of customers

An acquisition affects a large number of both companies' external partners: customers, suppliers, bankers and competitors. They all view the acquisition in a positive, neutral or negative manner and react accordingly. Many studies have stressed the negative perceptions of customers who are likely to break off their relationship with the buyer. The departure of big customers has a strong impact on the outcome of the transaction: it instantly diminishes the value of their supplier and can reduce to nothing the exploitation of synergies based on the prospect of product cross-selling to these customers. Retaining, reassuring and satisfying the demands of customers would appear to be of prime importance.

Another difficulty of a more technical nature has to be added to these five human problems: the merging of information systems.

Combining information systems

The information systems (ISs) of both partners are rarely compatible. In fact, the architecture and the functionality of an IS are modelled on a company's organization: structure, procedures, management practices, ... Consequently, the applications and functionalities of the IS are adapted to the organizational characteristics. Even if the standard equipment and software come from the same supplier, there will still be differences between the buyer's IS and the target company's. These differences, the changes to be made and the costs involved are rarely valued during the phase of hopes (Merali and McKiernan, 1993). In truth the task is complex; it requires the use of specialists from both companies and sometimes of external consultants. Depending on how the merger has been planned, the buyer can envisage a priori four solutions: select one

IS and impose it on the other organization, create a new IS, build interfaces that enable the two ISs to communicate or keep two autonomous ISs. Whatever solution is chosen, the acquirer usually needs to evaluate intermediary outcomes during the integration process. He wants to have reliable reporting tools and measuring instruments rapidly at his disposal (Gates and Very, 2001). Consequently, the systems are rarely kept totally autonomous. If we accept what executives tell us, the difficulties, the cost and the time necessary to implement changes are underestimated, causing initial forecasts to be more or less wide of the mark. The ability to resolve this complex problem effectively has an impact on the success of the acquisition.

These are the six major difficulties confronted by participants in the process, although this list is by no means exhaustive. The six problems are not completely independent of each other: for example, the loss of customers may lead some members of a demotivated salesforce to resign and give rise to uncertainty in others. Imposing an information system on a company could bring cultural resistances to light and create power games. In such situations, the different teams in charge of the integration will have to coordinate their actions if these difficulties are to be resolved.

The occurrence of problems

Obviously you would like to know in advance what problems you are likely to encounter in acquiring company X. Although it is impossible to foresee everything, you can nevertheless anticipate a large number of the difficulties.

To do that, we will start by ranking the problems into two categories according to the frequency with which they occur.[4] Three problems are almost systematic: ambiguities and individual uncertainties, power games and combining two ISs. Moreover, the first two are not specific to acquisitions, but are characteristic of any radical change within an organization. They will evolve throughout the reorganization process. The third problem is linked to the massive development of integrated management software packages, which cause a form of structural inertia in the face of large-scale change. Investments in information systems are heavy and for the most part irreversible. Figure 4.2 describes these effects. The solutions to these three difficulties need to be studied before the deal is closed (i.e.,

---

[4] Our line of reasoning here does not include cases of acquisitions that have been made for reasons of conglomerate diversification.

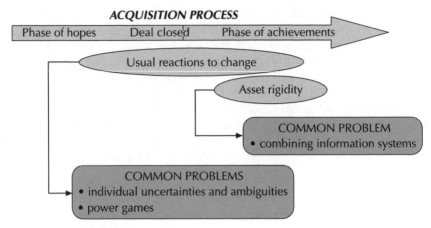

Figure 4.2   The difficulties commonly encountered.

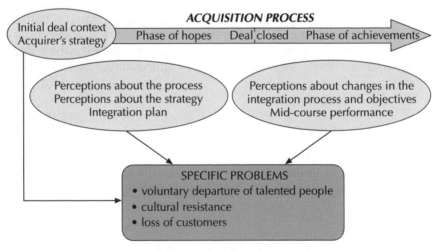

Figure 4.3   The difficulties sometimes encountered.

during the phase of hopes if the conditions of the merger allow you to do so).

The other three problems are not encountered as frequently. Their occurrence is linked to several factors: the initial context, the strategic plan, how the process is conducted, the integration plan, its implementation, external events, the early performances of the merger ... But it is above all, as Figure 4.3 illustrates, the interweaving of these aspects that gives rise to difficulties. Big differences in salary are a problem when the employees of both companies work together on similar tasks. The difficulty arises only when contact is made. Let's look at some other consequences of this interweaving:

- The acquisition of a company that was in direct competition with the buyer often leads to voluntary departures when the strategic plan includes a merging of teams. The salespeople who fought against their counterparts from the other company must collaborate with them from now. If the acquirer does not act beforehand to keep these people, there is a risk that they will leave the company when a new sales organization is put in place.
- A vertical diversification downwards puts the company in competition with its traditional customers; the renegotiation of contracts with these customers has to be well managed, otherwise there is a big risk of losing them.
- The acquisition of a foreign company to reinforce your international position in an industry may rely at first on the complementarities of the market to create additional value. Economies of scale in production are then neglected in favour of maintaining autonomy of operations. However, badly conducted negotiations or a buyer giving in to a heavily emotional atmosphere may lead to an acquisition for a price that is a lot higher than the true valuation of the company. In this case, the buyer will be tempted to alter his approach to the combination. He will opt purely and simply for an absorption, for only this will enable him to exploit all the synergies likely to justify the price and provide him with the value hoped for. Consequently, he will have to redeploy production forces and eliminate redundant posts. He might lose talented people because of this change of plan. If into the bargain he has acquired a successful company that is proud of its autonomy, its values and management practices, there is a risk that the change of orientation may trigger cultural resistance.
- Other factors also lead to modifications in the strategic plan or the integration plan during the process, with similar consequences to those mentioned above. For example, the strong decline of a cyclical market in the period after the acquisition, a very aggressive reaction from a competitor, weak profits recorded after the first months of integration, a pace of change that is slower than foreseen, ...

I could bore you stiff with examples. Let's make a general conclusion instead: the manner in which you start, the way relations between both sides evolve and the decisions taken by the buyer, all of these combine to eventually give rise to problems within the organizations. That being the case, it is possible to anticipate the occurrence of certain problems during the phase of hopes. By carefully studying the context of the acquisition, by examining the potential consequences that the implementation of the strategic plan could have, we can evaluate the probability of three specific problems emerging. Right throughout the negotiations, these probabilities are updated in relation to how the process is unfolding and to any alterations made in the provisional integration plan. To illustrate this method of analysis, we have gathered together in Table 4.1 information from the seven stories that make up this book. For each one, we have collected data concerning the context, how the process was conducted and the methods for combining the companies (strategy and integration plan). In a real situation, the analysis would be more precise than what is proposed in the Table, the aim of which is simply to point out a path to follow.

Thanks to this systematic analysis, the buyer acquires the capacity to take preventive action. Example: the strategic plan means that the target company has to radically review its orientations and you also refuse to maintain employees' salaries during the negotiations. Consequence: a real probability that talented people will leave. So, you meet the key people, examine their motivation in relation to the project, respond to their wishes as far as possible and communicate in a way that will reassure them and win them over ...

Since you have paid a high price, you decide in the end to merge the teams and the organizations rapidly in order to exploit synergies as soon as possible. Unfortunately, these choices are announced after the acquisition comes into effect and there is the threat of a collective rebellion of a cultural nature. So, what do you do? Keep some elements of their culture that do not in any way alter the manner in which the project is conducted. Organize formal meetings and encourage informal contacts so that everyone understands the values and practices of the other company. Prepare your teams and encourage them to collaborate with their counterparts. Use training and site visits to make people understand the realities, ...

Customers are not in favour of the acquisition project. Your subsequent decisions to standardize sales practices and reduce the salesforce could lead to customers deserting you: so, meet the major customers as soon as possible, explain your project, reassure, find solutions that satisfy each party, ...

Such steps do not guarantee success, for the scarcity of information and the subsequent occurrence of events that were not foreseen make it impossible to anticipate everything. Nevertheless, they are basic actions that can minimize those risks that are foreseeable. In addition, when no positive solution has been identified to avoid a difficulty arising, the buyer might be induced to abandon the transaction or to renegotiate the value of the project in the light of the obstacle to be cleared.

Table 4.1 Comparison of the seven acquisition stories

	Flight NA3365 to Morkousk	To conquer the world	The gold nugget	The Christmas present	Fateful encounters	The Meletev cocktail	Sabotage
Context variables							
Relative size of acquired company relative to the acquirer size	Equal	Smaller	Smaller	Smaller	Equal	A little smaller	Smaller
Prior economic performance of the target	Average	Average	Very good	Bad	Very good	Very good	Diverse types in the story
Nationality of companies: same (S) or different (D)	D	S and D cases in the story	S	S	D	D	S
Acquirer listed (L) or not listed (NL) on stock exchange	L	L	NL	NL	L	L	NL
Strategy: expansion (E), diversification (D) or vertical integration (VI)	E	E	E	VI	E	E	E, D and VI
Variables associated with process monitoring in the phase of hopes							
Initiator of the transaction: acquirer (A) or Seller (S)	A	S	A	S	A	A	A
Friendly (F) or hostile (H) transaction	F	F	F	F	H	F	Diverse types in the story
Too high a price	No	Yes	Yes	No	Yes	NS	NS
Poor negotiation	NS	NS	Yes	NS	NS	NS	NS
Variables associated with the phase of achievements							
Extent of synergies	Strong	Strong	Strong	Weak	Strong	Strong	Diverse types in the story
Type of integration: absorption (A), symbiosis (S), preservation (P)	A	S	A	P	S	A	Diverse types in the story

NS = not stated.

All things considered, the ability to anticipate and look for solutions is praiseworthy, and even more so if it is complemented by a capacity to notice precursory signals of emerging difficulties.

Summary

The successful management of an acquisition process means that the buyer has to ensure both the creation of the value hoped for and the preservation of both companies' initial value. All the analyses have to be updated permanently: not only the financial valuations, but also those concerning the strategic plan or the identification of major difficulties likely to be encountered. Certain problems appear very frequently and should be studied right from the phase of hopes. Others arise in relation to the context and the unfolding of the project: the probability of their emergence needs to be assessed in the course of time, in order to take preventive action if necessary.

Nevertheless, we should not forget one characteristic of acquisitions: efforts to anticipate events are necessary, but they do not guarantee against the discovery of a "skeleton" or the occurrence of an unexpected event. Anticipate, but remain vigilant. It would be a pity to go home in the evening and announce: "Honey, I've shrunk ... the firm!"

Chapter 5

Exploring the cultural dimension

5.1. STORY: FATEFUL ENCOUNTERS

Tomorrow will be a big day! The day that marks the official takeover of the Placom group. The tender offer had succeeded. Mathias Perth was happy and relieved that the marathon he had endured these last weeks was at an end. But, at the same time, he felt some anxiety. His financial director had shown him the figures to prove that the price offered per share was a reasonable one. However, Mathias would have liked to know more about the target company before closing the deal. Some questions remained unanswered. Why had it been so easy to convince certain shareholders? The synergies they had identified were beneficial on paper, but would they be easy to exploit? Although this mega-operation between Digit and Placom had been welcomed by the stock exchange, the purely economic and financial calculations did not bring Mathias the peace of mind he expected.

Simultaneously, 8,000 km away, Quentin Tarfel was thinking the same thing: tomorrow would be a big day! Christine, his communications director, had accepted straight away his invitation to dinner. "We've now known each other for three years," Quentin thought. "Since I was appointed head of Digit France. When I arrived, she was going through divorce proceedings. As she's now free, I'll have to grab my chance. I can't wait for tomorrow!"

How the merging process was handled

The takeover of the European company Placom by the American company Digit would give birth to the world number one in the field of cable communications equipment. Mathias Perth had instigated this manoeuvre. The Placom top managers had at first rejected his plan for a friendly merger. On the advice of their investment bank, Digit had then launched a hostile bid for the 60% of shares that were quoted on the London Stock Exchange. Mathias had taken his precautions. He had used his network of business contacts. He had negotiated skilfully with the main shareholders. Mathias, with help from his network, had been assured of their support. The operation had been prepared in secret to limit the risks of failure. Lawyers and bankers had worked relentlessly to ensure the success of the procedure. Placom had tried in vain to find a "white knight"[1]. A few shareholders had spoken out in public against the takeover bid. Several times Mathias had explained his strategy to journalists, financial analysts and government bodies. In the end, Digit had encountered few difficulties in getting control of the majority of its rival's capital.

The merger had also been the subject of an enquiry by the American and European anti-trust authorities. In the United States, the Federal Trade Commission and the Antitrust Division of the Justice Department were in favour. In spite of patriotic pressure exerted in favour of Placom's independence, the European Commission had considered that the merger did not constitute a constraint on free competition. In actual fact, the European and American authorities had invoked the principle of international courtesy, a cooperation and coordination agreement concerning the application of competition rules.

Mathias now had his hands free to organize the merger of the two groups. He had had a meeting with his senior management and external consultants to draw up a plan to implement the merger. Six fields of action were outlined:

- An in-house team would replace Placom's senior management team immediately. Their hostility to the manoeuvre was behind this decision. Digit's European chief executive was appointed as head of Placom and would stay there while the group still retained a distinct legal identity. He would pick his new management team himself.
- Digit's usual consultants would audit Placom's different units throughout the world. In six months' time, this mission should be completed.
- Three working groups were set up, each one composed of managers from both companies. The first group would work on the insertion of Digit's technological innovations into Placom's leading products. The

---

[1] A company making an acceptable counter offer for a company facing a hostile takeover bid.

second group would study how to extend Placom's successful productivity optimization methods to the whole organization. The third group would look at how to reorganize purchasing in order to negotiate a lower price for bigger quantities with suppliers. In other words, the objective for these teams was to plan the implementation of synergies. They had one month to accomplish their tasks and deliver an implementation plan. Each week, the team leaders would send in a report detailing the progress of their work.

- A firm of consultants was put in charge of designing the architecture of the new organization that would be set up. They had two months to come up with their first proposals.

- An internal team, made up of cost accountants, financial experts and computer specialists from both companies, was put in charge of harmonizing reporting procedures. They had one month to make their recommendations; the prime objective was not to make savings, but rather to obtain comparable information from both companies quickly.

- Finally, an internal and external communication plan was drawn up. Mathias Perth would be in the front line in order to arouse interest in his strategy and to explain the broad outlines of its implementation. A timetable was worked out. Mathias would speak to several different groups of people: employees of both companies, trade unions, operational managers, managers of foreign subsidiaries, shareholders, main customers, main suppliers, government bodies, bankers, financial analysts and journalists. In total more than 15 meetings in 40 days were planned in different parts of the world.

A month and a half later, Mathias made a first assessment of how things were going. The progress of the work was on schedule, but results were sometimes less than hoped for. Among the positive points, most of the teams working on the priorities were doing an excellent job. Placom's top managers cooperated willingly. It was a nice surprise for Mathias and his people. It seemed that others did not share the hostile position adopted by the top executives. Another reason for satisfaction: the new faces managing Placom had quickly found their marks and were proving to be very efficient. In addition, negotiations with suppliers would start in a month's time, with the target of achieving savings of 3% on purchases from the first year. This was the objective that had been established in the simulation exercises before the acquisition.

On the other hand, the teams in charge of studying the transfer of skills gave a pessimistic report. It was proving to be impossible in the short term to apply Placom's efficient methods to Digit. Placom had invested massively in its own version of ERP[2] three years before. Placom's internal efficiency was for the most part linked to the use of this ERP which provided integrated management of the company's activities. The achievement of a high degree of efficiency had required a large structural reorganization, which was Placom's strength today. Digit had also developed its own ERP, but they were two years behind Placom. This program was only at the testing stage. To make matters worse, the specialists from the two companies noted that they had both chosen technical solutions that were almost incompatible. One of the ERPs would have to be discarded, if they wanted to unify their systems. However, it was difficult to imagine abandoning Digit's ERP: tens of millions of dollars had been invested in this system which had multiple applications. If the project were halted, that would mean that these sums had been spent for nothing. The large number of colleagues involved in the project would find it difficult to understand this choice. Mathias and his management team decided to defer unification of the ERPs. They wanted to avoid too many changes.

"Let's first absorb Placom, then we'll modify our organization," Mathias had concluded.

The board of directors decided to freeze most of the investments devoted to the information systems. The two ERPs would cohabit for at least a year within the new group. As a result, Placom's distinctive skills would not be extended to Digit in the short term.

Another negative conclusion came out of the first analyses: some of Digit's innovations could not be transferred to Placom's products, because of basic differences in the design of the products. In addition, the research and development teams had totally different working methods, thus eliminating the potential for cooperation in the short term. Mathias Perth's apprehensions were proving to be justified: some of the synergies they had imagined did not exist. This was a terrible blow for Mathias, for it meant that the price offered per share was certainly too high.

"Good grief is there no end in sight to it all," Mathias thought. "The day before yesterday I was dashing around all day and night to conclude the deal. Yesterday I was still dashing around all day, sleeping at night in planes, to take the good word to our people and our partners. I'm fed up!"

Flying around the world had worn him out physically. He was exhausted and felt like dropping everything. However, some minutes later, he was his old optimistic self again.

"Okay, we paid a high price. Now, we'll have to find a way to justify this price."

---

[2] Enterprise resource planning, an integrated management software package.

Mathias summoned his senior management and his advisers to a crisis meeting.

The flames of passion . . .

"It's not possible, he's got his head in the clouds. He must be in love." Daphné, Digit France's personal assistant was tearing her hair out. For nearly two months now, her boss had been forgetting appointments, mislaying important dossiers and taking long lunch breaks. Daphné was looking for an explanation for Quentin Tarfel's rather dilettante behaviour. Her intuition was right. Since dining out together, Quentin only had thoughts for Christine, and she only had thoughts for him. They were like two teenagers in love. Quentin felt as if he was experiencing a second student life, all the more so as they had something in common from that period: they had both been to EDHEC, a graduate business school! Quentin had studied at the Nice site, three years before her. Christine had studied at the Lille site. Give or take a year, they could easily have met, as there were many exchanges between students at both sites. The two lovers often talked about these good old days and the near coincidence. However, they were careful to keep things secret at work.

Quentin thought of little else. He followed events going on at Digit with an air of detachment. First of all, he had learned about the success of the takeover bid from the press. The next day, confirmation had arrived from the USA via internal email. As usual in Digit, the employees felt that they were the last to be informed: a poor show for a company that worked in the telecommunications industry. Three weeks later, Quentin had been invited to the Netherlands to attend a mass rally. Mathias Perth in person had outlined his strategy in front of all the managers of European subsidiaries. There had been numerous questions about the integration of Placom. Indeed, up till now, Placom had been considered as the main rival of most of the European subsidiaries. From now on, the competitor would be part of the same company. Would Digit want to maintain competition internally or would the different teams be integrated? Would there be any redundancies? Instead of replying directly, Mathias explained that the integration plan would be ready in one month's time. He promised those present that they would be kept up to date about decisions and he managed to reassure his people.

When he got back to Paris, Quentin reported his boss's words to his employees. They would have to wait for decisions from the USA. A week later, he received a phone call from the manager of Placom's French subsidiary. The latter was worried about what they could expect in the near future. Auditors had been checking his company's accounts for the past week. Although he did not really like the person he was speaking to,

Quentin adopted an enthusiastic attitude. He explained that they would soon be informed of the choices of organization. They decided that in this period of uncertainty it would be better to show solidarity with each other. That was why, as soon as one of them learned something important, he would pass it on at once to the other.

In reality, neither man had much news to exchange during the month that followed. Quentin had no idea about the future reorganizations. Mathias Perth still had not informed the managers of the subsidiaries. Even journalists did not seem to have anything to go on. Quentin was not worried: in any case, he had Christine and that was all that mattered to him.

A drastic plan

The crisis meeting marked the start of a terrible week for Mathias Perth and his close colleagues. It was a big test for all of them and they were stressed at the thought of the consequences their choices might bring. Yet, it had all started off with a simple question: How were they going to get a return on their investment in Placom, so as to create value for their share-holders? The question remained unchanged, but what they knew had changed. Before the acquisition, the answer had been based on assumptions and hoped-for gains; today it was based on the real cost of the investment, real synergies, real resources and real figures. When he confided in those close to him, Mathias talked especially about additional investment costs, the absence of synergies and limited resources. No matter how they were worded, the internal investigations' reports brought unfavourable news every day. The picture they had imagined was far removed from reality. This emerging reality was now forcing them to alter their action plans noticeably. The internal mechanisms they had been counting on to create value were now a pipe dream!

Mathias was looking for the new equation, the "right" equation. His strategy consultants were put to work on this for five days. After two days, the management team and the consultants had to face facts: only one solution was possible. They would have to design a new configuration for their worldwide business activities by merging all the companies' units. This merger would be completed in a year and a half for the production sites and the sales departments. Combining research and Development teams would take two years. Although their working methods were different, researchers would be forced to cooperate as quickly as possible. At this price they could get a return on their investment in Placom.

The next two days were devoted to the reconfiguration of their business activities. Directors and consultants divided the world into five large regions of operations. For each region, they assessed the nature and size of changes to be implemented. They looked at three possible types of change: closing a site, combining the resources of two sites and creating new relationships between sites that had been retained. When a new allocation of resources for a geographical region was planned, the consultants and the human resources director assessed the consequences in terms of staff reductions. Western Europe represented the most difficult region to deal with: it was Placom's historic base and still accounted for 60% of its turnover; Digit had a presence in every country of this region, which provided it with 30% of its sales. Consequently, the choice of sites to be retained was tricky. In order to get things moving, Mathias decided on a procedure and the criteria. The sites that would close would be those that had the weakest financial performance: let the best man win! On the other hand, two rules to ensure fairness would be applied in this region: on the one hand, staff reductions would affect the same number of employees in each company. Employees whose site was to close would be offered relocation. On the other hand, 50% of the future directors of national subsidiaries would come from Digit and 50% from Placom.

On the sixth day, Mathias was able to design his new organization and the redeployment of resources on the map of the world. In the reorganization 8% of jobs would be lost. Encouraging results were obtained from simulation exercises on profitability. The Sunday was declared a day of rest.

The following week, Mathias and his people devoted their time to selecting those who would be in charge of each of the five regions and the directors of each subsidiary. The consultants checked the feasibility of the plan country by country. Indeed, they discovered that national regulations in some countries concerning employment or the modifications of work contracts blocked the implementation of certain solutions that had been thought up in the USA. Consequently, some major corrections had to be made to the initial plan.

Two weeks after the crisis meeting, Mathias felt slightly unwell. His doctor advised him to rest. For Mathias, this was impossible: he knew that another marathon was starting the following Monday. He was going to pick up his pilgrim's staff and travel to the four corners of the globe, delivering his message about the reorganization to all those who would be concerned by it.

"Is there ever an end to it?" Mathias wondered, as he filled his suitcase with medicines.

Paris in turmoil

The letter arrived from European headquarters: Quentin had been appointed as head of the Japanese subsidiary! All that was needed was his agreement and then the decision would be official. Quentin studied the letter for a moment.

"I don't believe it," he yelled. "I don't want to leave. Not at this point in time!" His shouting could be heard in the corridor and made Daphné, his secretary, jump.

"But what's the matter with him? Isn't he well? Perhaps things aren't going too smoothly with Christine."

The bell of Saint Sulpice church struck nine o'clock. Quentin asked Christine to come to his office. She immediately left her office, walked past Daphné who smiled at her blissfully and entered her favourite director's lair. Quentin explained the Japanese proposal to her. Christine turned pale. They agreed to discuss it further over lunch. She went back to her work, with a tear in the corner of her eye. As she went by, Daphné noticed Christine's distress and said to herself:

"Oh dear, what a pity. And they seemed to be getting on so well ..."

Meanwhile, Quentin phoned the European chief executive. The latter's assistant replied that he was not available as he had been transferred. The ex-general manager of Germany would be taking over the post tomorrow!

Quentin hung up, annoyed. Who could he turn to in order to discuss his situation? He tried in vain to contact the human resources department in the USA. Every manager in the company seemed to be busy today. He sent several emails requesting that someone call him back.

He was sending his latest message over the intranet when the phone rang. It was the head of Placom France. He had been appointed as head of Digit-Placom France and would be taking up the post in ten days' time. He would be in charge of merging the two French subsidiaries. The new company, Digit-Placom France, would occupy Digit's premises. Quentin congratulated him, but remained vague about his own future. His counterpart then explained to him the instructions he had received.

"I have to reduce the sales staff: 10 out of the 30 salespeople will have to leave, 5 from Digit and 5 from Placom. In addition, human resources will inform me soon of how to go about harmonizing the remuneration policies. As far as internal management is concerned, the two ERPs will run in parallel for the next six months. I'd like to meet you before you leave so that you can explain your organization and management methods. For example, I don't know your remuneration policy or your integrated management software package. Could we spend an afternoon together in the next few days?"

"Of course. What about next Thursday?" replied Quentin, while thinking to himself: "I must be dreaming! This stupid ass must have contacts in high places to get this job. Okay, I'll play the game and give him the information he wants, but I won't be telling him which salespeople to sack. He'll have to sort that out himself! And it'll be up to him to inform my people about these changes.''

Quentin could not understand this choice. It was his objective opinion that he was the better man. He had taken market share from Placom. His bosses and the main customers had a high opinion of him. This could not be said of Placom's general manager. He was considered to be fairly mediocre.

Quentin could not understand either why events were now accelerating after two months of calm. Overnight everything seemed to have changed completely. Heads were turning, some people were disappearing and others were suffering. Two days earlier, at the second mass rally organized by Mathias Perth for the profit centre managers, the former had indeed talked of changes in postings and the merging of subsidiaries. But nobody had thought that the reorganization would be as brutal and as drastic. The managers had imagined that the modifications would be progressive and would proceed smoothly. After all, this was how Mathias had always worked since he had been head of Digit.

At 11 : 30 a.m., Quentin had a phone call from Australia. It was the worldwide human resources director. Quentin had already met this man at various in-house events and liked his straightforward manner and considered him to be reliable. He listened to Quentin's questions and then described the process and the rules they had used to select the head of each subsidiary. He explained the difficulties they had encountered in dealing with the European region. The head of Placom France had been selected for reasons of fairness. Skills were not a decisive criterion, otherwise Quentin would have been chosen instead. They thought highly of Quentin's qualities; that was why, rather than having him manage a medium-sized sales operation, Digit's head office preferred to entrust him with the management of a strategic subsidiary, Digit Japan. It was the group's biggest subsidiary in Asia and they needed someone capable of increasing the speed at which it was developing. In addition to commercial outlets, this subsidiary also managed two production sites and had a dynamic research and development centre. In brief, Quentin could in all sincerity regard this offer as a big promotion. It was a reward for his loyalty and past efforts, and was a mark of the confidence the company had in his abilities. Somewhat flattered, but still dumbfounded, Quentin thanked his superior and asked for a few days to reflect.

Once the conversation was over, Quentin joined Christine in a discreet restaurant. He told her about the morning's events. The situation looked complicated and the two lovers worked out different scenarios as to the future. In the end, their options proved to be limited. Either Quentin accepted, or he would have to leave the group since there was no place for him in France. If he accepted, what could Christine do? Either she asked for a transfer and went with them, or she stayed in France and they sacrificed their relationship. Three additional variables were also considered: first of all, Christine enjoyed her work in the French subsidiary; second, her job could be at risk given the speed at which events were unfolding; third, and most importantly, they loved each other and did not want to separate. There were too many variables; Quentin and Christine could not come to a decision. It was too complicated. So, they simplified matters by retaining only two scenarios: either we stay in Paris, or we fly to Nagasaki. In brief, they broke up that day promising they would never break up.

Life in Nagasaki

Looking spruce Christine walked into Quentin's office.

"Are you coming? It's time for our Japanese lesson."

They had been following an intensive training course since their arrival eight months beforehand. Christine loved it: she was fascinated by the language and the customs. She had discovered a world that she liked a lot. She avidly read books about the Japanese people written by anthropologists. Quentin liked his new life, but could imagine staying only three or four years in this country. He missed Europe, France and above all Paris. Nevertheless, moments of nostalgia were rare compared with the moments of intensity they enjoyed together. In addition, Nagasaki was not as oppressive as Tokyo. They lived by the sea, in a villa provided by Digit-Placom. It was only 15 minutes from their offices. The Japanese subsidiary's head office was located in Omura City high-tech park, a suburb of Nagasaki, so that they could collaborate easily with ITCN (Industrial Technology Center of Nagasaki), a renowned research centre. Today, despite the novelty of his job, a novelty that he had underestimated, Quentin did not regret coming to Japan. Far from the eyes and the heart of Digit-Placom, he enjoyed a lot of autonomy in managing his subsidiary.

Christine and Quentin had decided to give the Japanese adventure a go. Quentin had laid down one sole condition for his departure: that Christine be transferred to the Nagasaki subsidiary. The human resources department had quickly agreed.

Christine would supervise relations with the other subsidiaries of the group. As Japan manufactured components for other Asian subsidiaries, there was a big flow of products and information between the various establishments. As requested, it would be a part-time post, thus leaving her with enough free time to discover and immerse herself in Japanese life. Through the *PlaneteEDHEC.com* website, she had contacted former students of the school who were working in Japan. Quentin and Christine had participated in various events organized by EDHEC alumni. Quentin had thus formed very close contacts with his compatriots who had been living for a long time in the land of the rising sun. They willingly gave him advice when he was confronted with a local management problem.

There had been no shortage of difficulties since he had taken up the post. His first action had been to call a meeting of his senior management team, 80% of which was Japanese. The only two Westerners on the team had arrived at the same time as Quentin and were also discovering the country. Faced with his lack of experience of Japan, Quentin had decided to capitalize on the Japanese executives' experience to make a success of the merger of the local Digit and Placom subsidiaries, and to work out and implement new strategic orientations. They knew their own country, the customers, the competition as well as the past history of their own subsidiary of origin, Digit or Placom. They were the best placed to design the future. Quentin's predecessor had selected these people, as Quentin had requested.

During the first meeting, Quentin talked about the group's common project and insisted on the need to adapt this project for the Japanese subsidiary. Then, in order to consolidate the merger and its potential in the months to come, he outlined a number of tasks and divided them among the directors present. There were no objections. Two weeks later, Quentin realized that the Japanese directors had not progressed a lot. It took him nearly a month to understand the reasons: on the one hand, the directors did not want to decide on strategy, which was supposed to be the big boss's job; on the other hand, the direct competition between Digit and Placom on Japanese territory during the last decade had left its marks and the directors from each camp had no desire to cooperate with the "enemy".

Consequently, Quentin's first months as head of the Japanese subsidiary were not easy. He found it difficult to decipher the thoughts that lay behind the enigmatic smiles and the polite greetings. He had to understand the difference between *honne* and *tatemae*, true intentions and appearances. Gradually, he got to grips with the art of the *nema washi*, or how to find a consensus without having a confrontation. He found the advice he got from the EDHEC network very useful in helping him to understand these cultural issues. He also employed a consultant in communications, an American who had lived in Japan for a long time, and who offered his services to the directors of Western companies. Working with this consultant helped him to improve his communication with the Japanese. Quentin now felt more at ease when he was chairing meetings.

Not everything was negative. The employees had a strong work ethic. The modification of remuneration policies went better than expected. Quentin was aware of the respect the Japanese had for him in person and of their strong loyalty to the company. The fact that he was learning their language also went down well and earned him even more respect. Another positive aspect concerned the merger: Digit and Placom were complementary as far as production was concerned. So, the factories were not affected by any relocations or reorganizations. Only simple exchanges of activities between them were implemented: a few product lines manufactured by Digit were transferred to the Placom factory and vice versa.

Distribution and sales did raise problems that were far more difficult to resolve. In brief, there were too many people in relation to the volume of products shifted. In addition, the respective salesforces were just recovering from a very long and damaging price war that their rivalry had engendered. Using methods à la japonaise, Quentin had to impose his point of view, overcome underground resistance, decide, convince. In France, he would have shouted, threatened, banged his fist on the table. This thought made him smile now that the problem was almost resolved. He acknowledged also that his job had been made easier by calling in a legal adviser, an expert in Japanese employment legislation, whose help was invaluable. This expert then worked on the merger of the purchasing departments. This did not concern many people, but it was still an important source of potential savings. The first negotiations with suppliers were held two months after Quentin arrived. They revolved around a renegotiation of prices in view of the volumes of supplies that Digit-Placom would be buying from now on. Quentin then launched a selection process for their future preferred suppliers.

Research and development activities were regrouped in Nagasaki. It took six months to complete the relocations and for everyone to settle in. In line with directives for the rest of the world, Quentin set a limit of two years for the first profits to be obtained. Achieving this objective would be a real challenge. In fact, each research team had its own philosophy that required particular forms of organization and methods of working. In addition, each one had invested its resources in different areas of innovation. The new research director's mission was not going to be easy. His first job had been to intervene urgently to reassure their partners at ITCN in Omura City. Preoccupied by the merger, most of the Digit researchers had neglected the work that was ongoing with their counterparts at the ITCN. The latter were now wondering if these projects would continue.

Some eight months after Quentin's arrival, most of the changes were taking shape. In three months' time, he would launch a project to harmonize procedures and management systems. Quentin did not think there was any urgency. He also believed that the harmonization would not be total: Placom, with its fine internal mechanisms, would retain some of its own ways of working. Indeed, he did not want to "break the springs". Nevertheless the in-house cost accountants had their work cut out at the moment to compare the data from Digit with that from Placom. The link-up between the two ERPs had to be done manually. Quentin had decided that Placom people would work on connecting the two systems. Christine would supervise this work.

So, day after day the merger was taking shape. However, Quentin was worried. First of all, he found it strange that the group was neglecting him so much. He had received very little support for the implementation of the merger. For example, no one from head office seemed to think about the problem of the ERPs, and yet it was obvious that it concerned most of the subsidiaries. Had the top management set other priorities? Or were there not enough in-house experts available to study this problem? Head office did not seem to be in a hurry to harmonize the reporting systems. Amazing! Quentin would like to have understood, but his questions went unanswered. He had simply noted that investments in information systems had been cut without explanation. The top management had also remained silent about the results of the post-acquisition audit. When Quentin arrived in Japan, the experts from the international audit firm had already visited. And since then, Quentin had had no news about the audit's conclusions. He had not received a report. In fact, after knocking on numerous doors at the American head office, he had given up and had decided to merge the two companies himself, regularly informing his superiors of important decisions and progress achieved. He found the attitude of top management strange. His colleagues in charge of other subsidiaries thought likewise.

His other worry concerned this year's results. In all probability there would be losses. The reorganization and relocation costs were higher than had been announced when he left France.

"They made very rough estimates," Quentin said to himself. To this increase in costs they had to add the reduction in turnover that was a consequence of merging two hostile salesforces. Some customers had also gone to the competition for some of their purchases to avoid becoming solely dependent on Digit-Placom. Quentin estimated that the volume of sales had declined by about 5%. And then, to cap it all, there was the damage caused by the recent price war, plus an increase in fixed costs. It was not going to be a fantastic year. In spite of the inefficiency of the management systems at their disposal, the accounting and finance departments were closely watching the evolutions and their repercussions on the subsidiary's results.

"*Sayonara!*" said the Japanese teacher, extricating Quentin from his worries. Christine, looking radiant, gave him a comforting smile.

Another world

Mathias was coming to the end of his three weeks in the convalescent home. He had paid little attention to his health in recent months, and he had suffered from a serious heart attack while working in his office. Since then, he had delegated a number of responsibilities to his senior management. As his doctor often said, he would have to take a back seat and think about himself for a change.

There had been many worries recently. Some of the subsidiaries had been confronted with serious problems. In France especially, the renegotiation of the remuneration policies had led to strikes. The stock exchange, when it heard about all this, punished the group and Digit-Placom shares lost 20% of their value in two days. The new general manager in France had not been as effective as they had hoped. His only contribution was to slow down the fall of the share price. Some subsidiaries were doing better, like in Japan. There, the reorganizations were progressing quickly and would soon bear fruit. Restructuring the head office and redistributing responsibilities had taken eight months to complete. They had had to negotiate the departure of some of their top executives, from both Digit and Placom. In fact, he had to retain some of the Placom people, if he wanted to maintain the internal dynamism that characterized this company. In particular he had entrusted the information systems department and management control to Placom people. These specialists would be in charge of extending the Placom ERP throughout the new group. The Digit ERP was condemned to disappear next year.

The head office was now reorganized, but the subsidiaries felt isolated. His last instruction before leaving for the convalescent home was for the policy of support and communication with subsidiaries to be revived.

Lying on his chaise longue, on a balcony facing the sea, Mathias was regaining hope.

"We are now in a different ball game. There are more than 100,000 employees in the group. I can't manage that on my own. Sadly, I'll have to delegate more and get others to travel all over the world in my place. But, with this acquisition, we've now entered another world."

The nurse brought him his tablets. Mathias gazed at her. They had already had a long discussion and seemed to like each other. He was a bachelor, but not a confirmed one, and she was just getting over a divorce.

"As she's now free, I'll have to grab my chance," Mathias thought. "All the more so as I'm leaving this place tomorrow."

He invited her to dinner for the following evening; she accepted straight away.

"Tomorrow will be a big day!" he said to himself.

At the same time in New York, at the head office of the investment fund that was Digit-Placom's main shareholder, the two top executives were wondering about the future of an American company with 150,000 employees and of which they possessed the majority of the capital.

"And what if we sent good old Mathias Perth to Chicago, once he's back on his feet? He will be the ideal person to manage the reorganization ..."

In Paris, Daphné was sitting at her desk, reading a postcard that Quentin and Christine had kindly sent her from Japan. There was a tear running down her cheek.

"Tomorrow, I hope it will be my turn," she said to herself.

5.2. NATURALLY, CULTURE IS TO BLAME

Section 5.1's story, "Fateful encounters", illustrates many of the ideas set out in the previous chapters. It complements the story "To conquer the world" (Section 2.1) for discussing geostrategy. It deals with the choices of men. It underlines the difficulties posed by a hostile manoeuvre where any preliminary investigation of the target is ruled out and the buyer is restricted to purchasing in a situation where information is scarce. It touches on the need to be able to anticipate events and to react during the process.

Let's use this story here to discuss the famous "clash of cultures".

Cultures

Too high a price and cultural resistance are of course *the* reasons nearly always put forward to explain failures a posteriori. Bringing together different cultures seems to act like a brake on the implementation of the strategic plan. The symbol of union within a company, culture acts as a channel for resentment in a situation of mergers and acquisitions. It is the same old refrain heard again and again every time there is a problem: every complaint, vindication, grumble is accompanied by its own reference to culture. Does it really deserve this much consideration?

Corporate culture denotes a set of values and standards of behaviour that are shared by employees and which create a distinctive identity for the company. The history of the organization, the personality of the top executives, national cultural influence, the industry and associated professional trades, management practices, all these shape this culture during the development of the company (Calori et al., 1989). In return, organizational culture influences practices and lines of conduct.

According to Hofstede (1980), culture is a "collective programming of the mind" (or of minds) which is difficult to modify. In particular, national culture, which contributes to shaping the culture of the country's companies, is too deeply ingrained from childhood for it to disappear easily. Berger and Luckmann (1967) explained how the conception of reality develops in each individual. The main part of this process of socialization takes place during the first years of life. The child is influenced by institutions that contribute to its education, such as family, religion or school. A group of native individuals from the same country thus share certain institutional experiences. The primary educational institutions just mentioned have a mimetic or normative influence on individuals or companies. Other institutions like the political, financial and legal systems of a country, known as proximate institutions, exert a more coercive influence on organizations by defining a structure and constraints that have to be obeyed. This is what Whitley (1992) studied. These institutional forces have been put forward as the reason for national differences between management practices. As it is difficult to change primary educational institutions, it is all the more difficult to alter the results of the socialization experienced during the first years of life.

Three levels are therefore superimposed: the individual, the corporate and the national. The individual has been socialized during his childhood, but also retains his own personality, which influences his line of conduct. A company that operates in one country only is thus made up of individuals with different personalities, even though they have all frequented common or similar institutions. In fact, the system of values developed internally is influenced by national identity and the personalities of individuals, in particular company executives.

These details must be considered when discussing cultural resistance in the context of an acquisition. As it happens the three levels are often interwoven: if it is a domestic acquisition, then different corporate cultures appear to be the issue; with a cross-border acquisition it is national cultures that are in opposition. In truth, the problem is more complex for we have to consider the interrelationships between levels and the fact that national culture is only one factor among others that contribute to shaping corporate culture. No research up to now has shown that the variance between national cultures was greater than the variance between organizational cultures. The only evidence is that individuals, and executives in particular, have experienced a process of primary socialization, with a strong national element, which has a strong influence on their visions of reality and their behaviour. The rest is of little importance. Would you like an example? Just read on.

The famous "clash" of organizational cultures

Let's study the simplest case first of all, the merger of two companies from the same country. The cultural clash comes from this meeting of two groups of human beings as different values and standards of behaviour come under the magnifying glass. This meeting of cultures is linked to the rise of cultural resistance, often in the company that has been acquired. This resistance blocks the reorganization and the exploitation of synergies. Consequently, the performance objectives cannot be achieved. Such is the general line of reasoning that we hear or read as an explanation a posteriori for delays or disappointing results. Many teams of researchers have taken an interest in cultural differences. They have tried to validate the assumption that the greater the differences, the higher the probability of failure. This research has produced mixed results: the link has not been clearly and systematically proved. Those researchers, whose work has validated the assumption, have advised acquirers to choose targets that possess a culture similar to their own. However, it is already difficult to find targets that correspond to the strategic ambitions and financial resources of the acquirer. So, it will be rare for the latter to introduce cultural criteria into his initial choice. In addition, when the target company is suggested to him by an investment bank, he receives a huge file of economic, financial and strategic information. As these initial documents are of a very tacit nature, they very rarely contain information about the target company's culture. Consequently, the recommendations made by some researchers are far removed from reality.

If it is a friendly acquisition, it is possible to study the culture of the target company, but only once the first contacts have been made and if the partner agrees. In practice, the objective of such an analysis would be to assess how to exploit synergies and merge the organizations. Its results, to my knowledge, rarely lead directly to the deal being called off. They might possibly swing the balance toward one company rather than another, in situations where the buyer has several options. So, a project could be adapted to take account of some perceived cultural reality, but selection of a company for a shortlist will not be based on cultural similarity.

In the same way, studies on national cultural differences have looked at the relationship between the success rate and the cultural proximity of the two companies' countries of origin. Here again, the results are fairly mixed and the link has not been systematically proved. One theory even takes the opposite view: the theory of the psychic distance paradox. We look at this on p. 113.

At both national and organizational levels, it is a distortion of reality to say that cultural differences will inevitably lead to a "problem of culture".

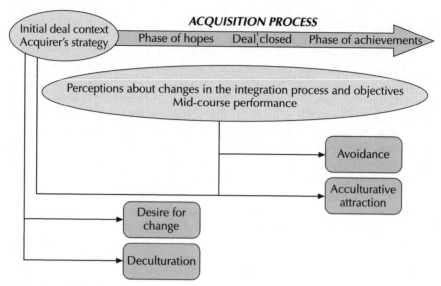

Figure 5.1   The cultural buffers.

In fact, there are four circumstances in which a clash of cultures may not arise. These four circumstances are outlined in Figure 5.1 and we will call them "buffers".

The buffers

One: Avoidance

For a clash to occur, the different cultures have got to meet. Let's imagine a situation: you have just acquired a company in a new sector of business for you and you retain its existing management team; all you do is transfer two of their experts with a particular skill to your company for one month. So, you have decided to maintain the acquired company's autonomy in management. In practice, apart from the two specialists who have been transferred temporarily, the people from both companies will never be in contact with each other. Even if they operate with different systems of values, the result will be the same: no conflict of styles.

Two: The desire for change

Let's examine what happens when cultures meet. For resistance to arise, we must assume that each group of people wants to keep its own identity and ways of working. Now, this is not always the case. A company could be up for sale because it is experiencing financial difficulties that the staff blame on the poor quality and performance of the management team. In this case, the employees might be ready to try another system of values and new practices: they have realized that their jobs and the survival of their company are at stake. A good example of this occurred in the 1990s. The American company Ingersoll-Rand acquired the French company Montabert, manufacturer of hydraulic equipment for mines and quarries. In spite of their very specialized know-how, Montabert's performances had been declining rapidly. Top executives held part of the capital and they could see their personal finances diminishing day after day. Ingersoll-Rand negotiated the acquisition of its great rival and outlined its strategic objective, which was to reposition the company using its specialized technological skills. A total reorganization was planned in order to improve internal efficiency. The acquired company would adopt Ingersoll-Rand methods of working. The buyer was hailed as a saviour by the majority of employees, despite the fact that there would probably be a reduction in staff. The new boss announced that 10% of staff would be made redundant. But in the end, Montabert would continue to live off its know-how. Employees whose jobs were safe were reassured and ready to modify their behaviour. They looked forward to the changes. The time had come. It was the start of a new life in a different universe.

Three: Acculturation

Let's now suppose that the cultures meet and there is no prior desire for change. Teams from both companies are going to have to merge, collaborate or coordinate with each other. We could indeed fear the emergence a priori of resistance when the buyer tries to impose common practices or when the takeover is hostile. In reality the confrontations are neither all black, nor all white. Reactions evolve during the process.

In order to understand this phenomenon, researchers have borrowed the theory of social movements from anthropology. This theory was developed by Berry (1983) who studied how immigrant populations acclimatized to their host countries. Berry introduced the concept of acculturation to describe the process of acclimatization. He identified a variety of forms of adaptation, ranging from total assimilation to integration (maintaining cultural identity but still accepting the local culture) to total rejection of the host country's culture. Beyond these types of acculturation, his research emphasized the notions of acculturative stress and acculturative attraction. Acculturative stress is the stress experienced by members of one culture when they are asked to interact with members of another culture and to adopt all or part of its ways of acting and behaving.

This acculturative stress is the basis for the classic premise concerning the link between cultural differences and the emergence of resistance. However, anthropologists have also identified the existence of an acculturative attraction in migrants, when certain ways of acting and behaving which exist in their host countries find favour with them. Following in the footsteps of Nahavandi and Malekzadeh (1988), pioneers in this field, Very et al. (1996) transposed these notions to the context of international acquisitions. We found that the existence of an acculturative attraction was linked to post-acquisition performance. In our sample of acquired companies, French firms that had been bought by Americans felt a stronger cultural compatibility than those bought by French people. It was the same for the British with regard to foreign or domestic acquirers.

Big changes give rise to ambivalent interpretations of the situation (Perret, 1996): confronted with new values and behaviour, people can feel stressed by some cultural elements and attracted to others. The discovery of a new world rarely proves to be negative in its entirety. New practices or values can attract. Things were fine before, now they are even better. Judgement, individual or collective, is relative to past experiences. It evolves during the merger, depending on contacts, on what the acquirer does and on the results of first collaborations. Enthusiasm is mingled with regrets. Cultural resistance will only arise if the stress felt by everyone is stronger than the acculturative attraction. Such is the conclusion that comes from this theoretical approach.

Like the crew of a space rocket, we will hesitate between the gravitational pull of earth from where we originate and the gravitational pull of the moon to where we are being asked to go. What will this new world be like? Will we miss the old world? It's up to those who rule the new world to attract us toward their universe.

Four: Deculturation

A temporary work agency experienced four successive reorganizations in seven years as a result of changing owner several times. The manager in charge of integration for the last buyer noticed the damage done: no resistance from the employees, but no enthusiasm for the new strategic plan. They continued working normally and appeared indifferent to the situation as long as there was no threat to their jobs. In brief, they came to work so as to have a salary at the end of the month and they simply went home when their day's work was finished. Changes were indeed put in place, but they had to be forced through in the face of the employees' passivity. Why should an employee put a lot of effort into the development of his company when there could easily be another change of orientation in the near future? If employees are to be motivated and rallied behind a project, they have to believe in its stability, that it will really happen.

This is a true story and it makes us wonder about the damaging effects of the proliferation of mergers and acquisitions in certain business sectors. The concept of culture may disintegrate if owners do not stay long enough. In this temporary agency, the employees experienced deculturation (i.e., they lost their bearings): their initial organizational culture disintegrated with all the changes and they adopted new values superficially, without really immersing themselves in these values. They maintained their working habits and favoured team solidarity more than individual changes in working style demanded by the last owner. Work is not considered as something of importance in their lives. They do the minimum just to keep their jobs. Can we still talk about culture?

Deculturation, which is the loss of a collective identity, incites people to avoid opposing the new owner as much as possible, but without serving his interests at the same time. So, this is the fourth reason an acquisition does not systematically result in cultural resistance.

The nature of collective resistance

Of the four circumstances mentioned above, acculturation tends to prove that confrontation with another culture creates phenomena of stress and attraction. Viewed from this perspective, it does not matter in the end that the cultures are similar or different. It does not matter? The answer is "no", differences are important, particularly differences between national cultures that, as previously mentioned, are rooted in our experiences of local institutions. Thus, culture's role in acquisition success remains complex and challenging. Understanding culture's role requires us to look at both acculturation processes and the extent of cultural differences. Let's explore the nature of collective resistance by adopting the acquirer's viewpoint. The real question for the buyer is not one of differences or of acculturation: it concerns the identification of difficulties likely to be encountered, and that could block or slow down the merging process. Employees can apply various brakes to an acquisition process. Figure 5.2 gives us an overview of this.

Initial hostility and resistance to change of ownership

First of all, there is a lot of rubbish talked about cultural resistance. Relations between staff can deteriorate for two other reasons: a hostile takeover and the whiff of past hostility. When the buyer acquires his target through a hostile takeover bid, he does so without the owners' consent. Consequently, an aggressive takeover bid like this can cause strong

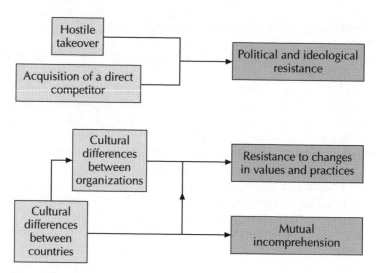

Figure 5.2 Collective resistance.

reactions in a target company that does not wish to negotiate. The employees take a dislike to the buyer and focus their resentment on him. They look for a white knight to come to the rescue. A real fight commences. If the takeover bid succeeds, the new owner is considered to be an unscrupulous conqueror. The target company rejects its new masters, either for their methods or for their domination. In fact, the confrontation is more political and ideological than cultural.

The other case concerns mergers between companies that were direct competitors. Just imagine: you have always wanted to take market share from company X. Your salespeople complain about the denigration of your products by company X. As you have no other choice, you sell your company to X. There is still deep-rooted resentment and the teams may refuse any collaboration with the old enemy. There are more and more conflicts. The best people leave. The problem is ideological.

So, not every collective resistance is cultural. It is an important distinction because appropriate solutions to conflicts and resistance are related to their nature. Communications, decisions and actions will all have to be adapted. The cure depends on the illness.

Cultural differences between organizations and resistance to internal change

Do differences count for anything? Yes, they do: cultural differences can generate resistance. This is the case when the acculturative stress is stronger than the attraction, when cultures collide and when the culture of the company acquired is well liked, ... at least, all things considered, fairly often!

Open conflicts, strikes and other events are the active forms of resistance, although employees can also choose to leave. Conflicts include a cognitive side (opposite judgements and viewpoints) and a very strong affective or emotional side (rejection, distrust, suspicion or insecurity with regard to the other company). This can lead to unfortunate results. In fact, whereas cognitive conflict is beneficial for progress, affective conflict harms the efficiency of work (Jehn, 1997). Other forms of resistance are passive, like working to rule, a voluntary decrease in productivity or adopting a position of wait and see in relation to the project. This type of resistance evolves with the course of time, according to events, the acquirer's actions and the performances achieved: perceptions change and cause new types of reaction.

The most robust active opposition often arises over trivial matters: "the other company has taken our parking places!" or even "the acquirer has moved the staff rest room without consulting us!" These apparent problems can hide a much deeper malaise. The trivial matter is in fact the open expression of hidden frustrations that have accumulated: the explosion occurs when the pressure becomes unbearable.

It is of course possible to iron out such difficulties. This involves rallying everyone from the start behind a common project, then presenting or negotiating an integration plan acceptable to everyone and which gives a foresight of future cultural evolutions: either retaining for the most part distinct cultures, imposing the buyer's culture or creating a common culture using the values and practices of both companies.

In theory, when it is a question of imposing or creating, the solutions to be employed are well known: listening to problems, communication, site visits, training in intercultural management, teamwork projects, the eventual definition of new values, retention of the best practices from each company, mixing groups through the sharing of space, appraisal and reward systems that encourage collaboration, ...

In practice, resolving cultural differences proves to be more complicated. We must remember that the buyer is acting in a situation where information is scarce. He is also under a strong pressure of time to achieve the expected performance objectives. He starts with a lack of information about the culture of the acquired company. Rarely does he have the time needed to study this culture and to lead the intercultural process efficiently. In reality, the acquirer has to arbitrate between the quality of the process and respecting deadlines. The risk of a strike is increasing: so, let's take time to dispel this malaise that might have disastrous repercussions on the value creation project. The staff are fairly unhappy but are cooperating: so, let's quickly put in place the organization we had planned; too bad if some of them leave. Arbitrating is a tricky business: the least signs of resistance need to be analysed, as well as the contingent risks. That is why the management of cultural resistance can prove to be exceptionally difficult.

National cultural differences and misunderstandings

The existence of cultural differences poses another problem, one that is particularly salient in the case of foreign acquisitions. In view of the fact that the people from the two countries have experienced different processes of primary socialization, it is logical that management practices and methods of organization should reflect, at least in part, these institutional roots. The buyer's people are brutally confronted with another conception of reality when they acquire a company in a new country. And, it is the same for the employees of the target company. The meeting of these two worlds does not necessarily create resistance. It can arouse curiosity or attract, as our research into acculturation has already shown. It does pose, however, problems of mutual incomprehension. This difficulty was mentioned a lot by executives who responded to a survey carried out with David Schweiger into cross-border acquisitions (Very and Schweiger, 2001).

This problem presents a worrying facet: much water will flow under the bridge before people will work together efficiently. In order to exploit the sharing of resources and transfers of skills, the acquirer will have to act beforehand. He has to ensure that employees in contact with their counterparts understand the latter's behaviour, decision-making and methods of working. There will be a proliferation of study seminars, training courses and informal meetings. Consequently, when the acquisition brings together two different populations whose values and behaviour are deeply rooted in their own native soil, the implementation of the project will require time. This is certainly a basic distinction with domestic acquisitions or acquisitions in a country where the buyer has long experience of the resources deployed locally.

Leaving aside financial considerations, this problem of mutual comprehension does present one positive facet for the players: what could be more exciting than discovering another culture, others ways of acting and behaving? The enrichment is not just of a purely financial nature.

Expatriates are doubly exposed to this phenomenon: they discover at the same time the culture of the company and that of their host country. In fact, outside working hours, they are immersed in the local way of life. In Section 5.1's story, "Fateful encounters", Quentin Tarfel and Christine confront this double novelty with curiosity and attraction. The communication difficulties posed by two totally different languages made the task all the more arduous. Quentin needed six months to grasp a few basic principles of Japanese management and to begin to appear credible. But his apprenticeship was only just beginning.

International: The psychic distance paradox

Misunderstandings may lead us to think that it is easier to acquire in a country that is culturally similar. The more similar the cultures, the more the chances of success increase. Many studies into the internationalization process have started from such a premise. However, recent results invalidate this: the proximity of cultures does not appear to be linked to success (O'Grady and Lane, 1996). The researchers explained this phenomenon by the "psychic distance paradox". This paradox means that operations in countries that are psychologically close to each other are not necessarily easy to manage, because the perception of similarity prevents executives from apprehending critical cultural differences. In other words, a perception of relatively strong, global similarity leads to a neglect of in-depth investigations. The easier it looks, the harder it is in reality!

Valid for every mode of development abroad, this theory can therefore be applied to acquisitions. Faced with a culture that is radically different, it is indeed very difficult to overcome misunderstandings. The investment is costly, at least in time and human energy. Understanding others requires a lot of attention and a desire to learn. Conversely, when the buyer thinks that he is in control of the cultural context, this confidence – or overconfidence – is likely to play tricks on him, for the need to learn has not been understood.

This theory of the paradox therefore challenges the link between the extent of cultural differences and the achievement of financial objectives. For the acquirer, it underlines above all the need to challenge presuppositions and to be vigilant in the face of novelty, whatever relative degree of novelty there is. Larsson and Risberg (1998) suggested that awareness of cultural differences provides a better explanation of research results than the simple existence of differences. Many executives nowadays have understood this and encourage their troops to learn and to understand. Thus Carlos Ghosn, the Renault director who became head of the Japanese company Nissan in 1998, considered cultural differences to be a strength, an asset that would serve the global strategic plan defined by the new group. Such positive thinking, linked to a number of concrete actions in the workplace, was beginning to bear fruit in 2000 (Emerson, 2001).

Summary

These details, which were intended to provoke thought, aim to show that the cultural problem is often skimmed over. The brief outline of the problem that we usually get, which associates the meeting of two different worlds with a harmful clash, is partly erroneous. When this does occur, it covers a wide variety of situations, each one necessitating an appropriate solution. However, whether there is resistance or not, the acquisition of a company in a new country exposes people to comprehension and communication difficulties. Consequently, getting people to collaborate quickly, who were born into different environments and who are used to their company's own way of working, does remain a major issue.

Chapter 6

Using experience, but maintaining vigilance

6.1. STORY: THE MELETEV COCKTAIL

"As you know our chairman very well, do you think you could convince him to appoint me as head of our US operations?"

Ronald looked down at the glass of champagne in his hand. Then he looked up again and stared at his colleague. "So, now we're getting down to the truth," he said to himself. He waited a moment before answering.

"Okay, Bill, I'll back your application, but, in exchange, I want George and Al back in my team. I need their skills to manage the implementation of the new reporting system. I'll have a word with the chairman about you as soon as I get a chance. But, I can't promise anything."

"Thanks, Ronald. That's kind of you. I'd really love to get the job. You know that my wife Hillary is ill. That's why I want to stay in Phoenix. The climate suits her and the medical facilities are wonderful. I'm not sure I'll find the same in another part of the world. If we had to move, it would dent her morale. And that's what I want to avoid."

"I know, I know. But, as you can imagine, it's a complex problem. Relocating people and resources within the new organization is a real headache. The board is spending a lot of time on the subject. Besides, we still haven't worked out the criteria for choosing the 12 new area general managers. Some directors want it to be split evenly, six ex-Meletev and six ex-Brak. Others are insisting that we select the best person for each post. That's all I can tell you for the moment. But trust me, I'll put in a word for you. What about George and Al, is it possible?"

"Listen, if I get the job as head of US operations, I'll send them back to you. In any case, if I get the job, they'll not be working for me anymore; so, it won't pose a problem. Cheers!" he said raising his glass.

Bill and Ronald drank to each other's health. The general hubbub drowned the clinking of their glasses. Ronald moved away from Bill toward the buffet where he nibbled a few petit fours. "What a hypocrite. It's because his lover lives in Phoenix that he wants to stay. He doesn't care about his wife. And, he's very ambitious. He's capable of stealing my job someday." Ronald did not fear for his future; he had his chairman's confidence and was convinced that the merger could only increase his level of responsibility. He climbed onto the small platform where the two chairmen had given their speeches an hour earlier. Then he looked down on the room.

The cocktail party was to celebrate the friendly merger between two world giants of the telecommunications industry: the American company Meletev had just acquired the German company Brak. The contract had been signed and the official announcement made that morning. Both groups' top managers had been invited to this reception. There were about one hundred executives and directors gathered together in the main lounge of the Phoenix Hilton, chatting, laughing and congratulating each other. These people now managed a group with a turnover of $34 billion.

The atmosphere was rather cheerful, even if the employees did tend to group together by company. Ronald noted that the Brak managers were standing and chatting by the big bay window overlooking the swimming pool, whereas most of his colleagues were standing in the centre of the room. Suddenly Ronald felt a hand tugging at the bottom of his trousers. He looked down and, as his face turned crimson with embarrassment, he exclaimed: "Stela! What are you doing? Let go of my trouser leg! Someone will notice."

"Ronald, you are being bashful! Come down off your pedestal and come and get me a drink," retorted the Meletev human resources director.

Ronald and Stela

"So, how is my favourite financial controller?"

"Stela, stop flirting with me. I'm fine. I'm just a little tired after the negotiations of these past months. And you, my dear?"

"Well, everything's fine. Did you know, Ronald, that Brak is the 50th acquisition I've participated in since I joined Meletev seven years ago?"

"Congratulations. I think I'm on my tenth one."

"The 50th one has to be celebrated! Ronald, serve me another glass of champagne."

Ronald did so. The two friends smiled at each other and clinked glasses.

"Come on! Down the hatch!" said Stela, immediately putting her words into practice.

Ronald felt obliged to follow. Then he resumed the conversation.

"After 50 transactions, I can imagine that working on a merger has become routine for you."

"You're wrong, Ronald. Each case is unique. Take Brak: we've never acquired such a big company before. Moreover, they've got skills in fibre optics that interest us; we'll not be able to impose our practices on them in case it scares off their most talented people. We'll have to take account of their opinions when it comes to organizing the integration. I didn't have as much freedom as I had in previous transactions. In addition, it's our first acquisition in Germany, where we don't even have a sales operation. In brief, we knew nothing about Germany."

"You mean German culture?"

"Not only that. The problem is more complicated. Corporate legislation and employment laws are different; there is also the role played by the company in relation to its *Länder* and in relation to the German state; the trade unions have a particular role; the accounting systems and the tax regulations are also particular. In brief, the whole acquisition process, from the first contacts right up to today, had to be amended to fit in with the institutional context. Cultural differences appeared during the negotiations, and these will be accentuated in the future as we move forward hand in hand. In Brak's case, we encountered problems of style we had never met before: we needed help to decipher German accountancy. We weren't sure how to go about buying the shares of a company, the majority of which were quoted on the Frankfurt Stock Exchange. We wondered if we had any managers in Meletev capable of managing operations on the German soil."

"So each case is different ..."

"No, Ronald, I wouldn't say that. After all, we have managed to write a guide to handling the acquisition process. After every acquisition, we record our remarks, our successes and failures, and this enables us to amend our practices so as to be even more successful the next time. In spite of differences in context, there are things that are constant in the change process. Certain difficulties are always encountered; others depend on the initial context and what the buyer does. You have to feel the atmosphere. Personally, I think that humility and thoroughness are the two main qualities required by my role. I work the same way an airplane pilot does before take-off. The pilot does the same checks for the thousandth time in his life; if he isn't thorough, he may endanger the lives of his passengers and crew; if he isn't humble, he will take off feeling that nothing can escape him and that he has total control of the situation. That's just as dangerous. I sincerely believe that with experience you acquire tacit knowledge that can't be described in a manual. And it's this knowledge that is the most important thing."

"So you don't always integrate each company in an identical way ..."

"Exactly."

"For example, in Brak's case, did you harmonize the remuneration and compensation policies the same way you did in past acquisitions?"

"Yes. It wasn't easy to reach agreement, considering the national differences. Nevertheless, once the decision was taken to regroup all the employees inside one American company, we've been able to make progress on the harmonization. In one month's time, every Brak employee will receive a dossier specifying his role and the name of his immediate superior. It'll also describe his holiday entitlement, bonus plans, the retirement scheme and the social security cover provided by Meletev. By the end of this week they'll all have a personal email address and a direct link to the Meletev Intranet. They'll also receive business cards with their names on them. As the bonus plan and the social security cover are better than that provided by Brak, those employees who were asked for their opinions about the changes responded favourably. In any case, our arrival in Germany has been an open secret for the last three months. And Brak has welcomed this. If you need proof, just look at how the departure rate of employees has gone down in the last quarter. I don't know if it's related to us, but believe you me, I was very proud to announce to our board that Brak employees were no longer leaving the company!"

"That's incredible!"

"My team and I have spent a lot of time in the Brak factories these past months. We analysed their organization and their working methods. We had many discussions with the staff, often in the form of individual interviews. We outlined our integration philosophy and expressed our wish to maintain an esprit de corps in Brak. These efforts have perhaps paid off."

"Of course they have, Stela. You're being modest, but I'm convinced that you do your job exceptionally well."

"Ronald, you flatter me. Here, give me another glass of champagne instead of talking nonsense." Ronald took two glasses from the buffet table and gave one to Stela.

"By the way, Stela, how did the negotiations about exchanging shares end up? I haven't had any information recently, but I know it was something that could have caused the whole operation to fail."

"It wasn't easy. It certainly contributed to raising the price of the transaction. In the end, Brak managers who owned shares in the company got 2.44 Meletev shares in exchange for one Brak share."

"That's enormous! They must have been delighted with the transaction."

"Yes, it's a very advantageous exchange. I was there when it was announced to the senior management. You should have seen them! They all grabbed their calculators and tapped furiously. Then, we saw smiles on every face. I remember one young engineer who's in charge of a research center. He possesses 20,000 shares in Brak. When he realized that the exchange would push the value of his share capital up to more than 3.2 million dollars, he couldn't get over it. He did the calculation more than ten times."

"In the end, everyone is happy in this story."

"Let's say the majority. For the salesforces, the merging of teams is going to mean staff reductions. The salespeople know this, so the atmosphere is tenser. The salesforces will have to be reorganized quickly to stop the situation getting worse."

So, if I have understood well, you're still going to be hard at it in the next few months."

"Correct, my dear Sherlock Holmes. Can you get me another drink, please?"

"Stela, you've had enough."

"Ronald, when you've had to live for more than a month in Munich as I had to during the October beer festival, you'll be so sick of beer that you'll appreciate the gentle bubbling of this French nectar."

Ronald suddenly felt a hand on his shoulder. He turned around.

Ronald and Gunther

It was Michael Dee, chairman of Meletev. He turned toward a third person, two metres tall and easily carrying his 120 kilos.

"Gunther, you've already met Stela. Let me introduce Ronald Granea to you. He's our chief financial controller. Ronald, this is Gunther Plitsch, chairman of Brak."

The two men said hello. Mike Dee went on:

"Gunther, you have in front of you one of the rising stars of our company. Ronald is young, dynamic and full of talent. He'll be in charge of the information systems project."

"Mike, you're giving me too much credit," Ronald declared.

"So, I'll leave the two of you together and I'll pinch Stela; I've two or three important subjects to discuss with her."

Ronald smiled at Mike, and then spoke to Gunther.

"So, Herr Plitsch, what do you think of the changes?"

"Everything's going wonderfully well. I think the merger will enable us to reign supreme in our market in two years' time. In combining our forces we're increasing our strength. The Germans feel that they're losing one of the flagships of their economy, but, frankly, my shareholders and I think we didn't have the necessary financial resources to survive for ever in a global industry that is in the process of concentrating. From the moment Meletev gave the government guarantees concerning the preservation of jobs in Germany, national resistance crumbled. I'm convinced that together we'll succeed."

"Fine. May I ask you a personal question? Of course, you're not obliged to answer: what post will you occupy in the new organization?"

"I can give you the answer. It's not a secret. Mike has offered me a seat on the board and I have accepted. As I'm only a few years off retirement, I don't mind taking a back seat. It'll do me the world of good."

"So, you're going to move to the USA?"

"No. I love my country and I will go on living there. How could I live here? You can't even find a decent beer!" exclaimed Gunther in a thundering voice. Both men laughed out loud. Gunther took a handkerchief out of his pocket and wiped his eyes.

"I'll come to Phoenix for board meetings and when my services are needed. I'll continue at the same time to supervise business in Germany for one year."

Ronald took a liking to Gunther. He knew that Dee trusted his counterpart totally, and he could see why.

"And you, Herr Granea, tell me how you are going to join up the information systems."

"First of all, I'll not be doing it on my own. I'll be working in close collaboration with my counterpart in your company and with the two financial directors. We're going to set up a team that'll include IT specialists, then work out a budget, share out the tasks and set deadlines. We should have a unified reporting system in one month's time. That's the priority. Then we'll work out the details of how to convert the accounting systems and afterwards the cost accounting. At the same time, another team will finalize the creation of a common intranet for both companies. This should be operational the day the merger takes effect."

"It appears that you're going to use modules from our ERP to manage relations with customers and suppliers ..."

"That's correct, we asked consultants to do an audit of both systems. They recommended a mixed solution and will help us to implement it. The way you managed your databases was excellent and remarkably efficient."

"Thank you for your compliments, Herr Granea. We invested millions of dollars in our system, and I think my people would have been upset if we had abandoned it completely after the merger."

"We also invested heavily in this area. And I think that some of Meletev's IT managers will not be as happy with the choice."

"Fine, that's enough talk about work for this evening. I'm delighted to have met you. Let's have a glass of champagne to toast our meeting. What do you think?"

"With the greatest of pleasure!" replied Ronald hypocritically. His mind was starting to get fuddled with drink.

Both men raised their glasses.

"It still doesn't beat a good beer. That's the downside of globalization!" Gunther remarked. Both men laughed.

"*Prosit!*"

"*Prosit!*"

They drank slowly. Ronald tried discreetly to find a potted plant into which he could empty some of his champagne. Unfortunately there were none nearby. So, he decided to resume the conversation to avoid having to drink.

"Look at how people are spread around the room. The Brak people are not really mingling with their colleagues from Meletev."

"Correct, Herr Granea. That's because the Germans found out that the buffet near the swimming pool was better than the one in the main lounge", Gunther joked.

"Or because Rot Beer is being served by the swimming pool!" retorted Ronald.

Both men laughed again. Then they clinked glasses for the second time.

"It won't need a lot of time for everyone to get to know each other. But I'm counting on the lovely Stela to help these people accept and collaborate with each other. She's really exceptional."

"She's very competent."

"What's more, when she came to Munich, she was able to try real beer and real sauerkraut. We took her to the October beer festival. She really liked our food and she loved our national drink."

Ronald smiled discreetly, remembering what Stela had said to him half an hour earlier. "She's certainly a diplomat . . . ," he said to himself.

"I'm afraid I'll have to leave you now. I'll have to rejoin the swimming pool buffet fan club. I am delighted to have met you."

"The pleasure has been all mine. See you soon."

Gunther moved away. Ronald then saw Mike and Stela coming toward him.

Ronald, Stela and Mike

"Ronald, Stela will help you select the Brak people who will work with you on the information systems."

"Great. We've already recruited the managers, but we still have to select the IT specialists. I think the managers already involved should help us choose them. They know their people better than we do."

"That's what I intend to do," Stela replied. "I'll provide the logistical help you'll need for the contacts and the interviews."

"Perfect. We'll have to start work next week if we want to keep to our schedule. Are you free?"

"Ronald, you shouldn't ask a question like that in public!" retorted Stela.

Ronald turned red. Mike laughed. Stela smiled.

"Yes, I'm available ... for work, of course!" Stela said.

"Ronald, I'm counting on you," interrupted Mike. "We must have a common, reliable reporting system as soon as possible. It's the information base that is the most important thing from a strategic point of view. With such a tool at our disposal, we'll be able to take decisions, monitor our performances and communicate our results to the financial markets. We've created six teams that are working on six key areas vital for the success of this acquisition, but I consider that your team has a crucial role to play in the first months of the integration. Just as Stela's team has to keep people committed right throughout the process. If you encounter the slightest problem that needs me to intervene, don't hesitate to contact me."

"Thank you for your confidence in me, Mike," Ronald replied, "and I'll phone you if necessary. I've got two priorities: the reporting system and creating the database for the six projects. The database will enable you to monitor each project from day to day. I've delegated the development of this tool to the IT people. You'll find in it each team's objectives, the main stages of the project, the names of the employees involved, the budgets, money already spent and the progress of each task updated daily. It should be useful if we have to make adjustments in case of delays or resistance."

"An excellent initiative, Ronald."

Stela then spoke. "Talking of interventions, I've got a suggestion. Mike, that speech that you've just made with Gunther Plitsch, you should give it to the Brak employees as soon as possible."

"Gunther and I have already decided to do that. Next week I'm flying to Germany and we're going to go round the factories. I think you should come with us. You could analyse the reactions and see if any of them are uncertain as to the future."

"I will already be in Germany. I'll look at my diary tomorrow morning and let you know when I'm free. I also think we should have a meeting with the Brak union leaders in their French factory in Nancy. The preservation of jobs is a major concern in France. The fact that the head of

Meletev has made the effort to come in person and guarantee the security of jobs would be worth a lot more than any written communiqué."
"We'll try and make a detour through France. But, that's enough talk about work, let's change the subject. Well now Stela, it appears that you're a great lover of beer! So Gunther tells me."
Ronald smiled discreetly. Then he roared with laughter when he saw Stela turn red as she mumbled a reply. He could feel his mind becoming more and more fuddled with the drink. The champagne was going to his head. He decided to get some air, made his excuses and moved off toward the swimming pool.

Everyone gets soaked

With his hands in his pockets, Ronald stood at the edge of the swimming pool, looking up at the sky. It was a magnificent night, with moonlight and hundreds of stars. The autumn breeze gently caressed his face. "Isn't life wonderful!" he thought to himself.
"Ronald, I've got to talk to you."
Ronald turned around. Not Bill again! On second thoughts, life would be wonderful without Bill ...
"Ronald, I've just found out that Jack Stone and one of the Germans are in the running for the US job. You've really got to do something for me."
"Listen, I told you that I'd put a word in for you in due course. What more can I do?"
"Introduce me to our chairman."
Ronald was taken aback. No way was he going to ruin his good image with Mike for this scheming rat. "Bill, there's no point. The fact that you were invited to this cocktail party shows that you're part of the company's elite. So, you can go and speak to Mike on your own ..."
"You see, you call him Mike. I don't. For me, he's still Mr Dee."
"So? All you have to do is call him Mr Dee. He'll reply using your first name, and after that, you can call him Mike."
"Why don't you introduce me? It would be a lot simpler."
Ronald suddenly saw Stela coming over. He had an idea.
"Wait a moment, Bill, I'll introduce you to Mike's favourite person. Do you know Stela?"
"Only by name."
"You can speak to her openly, she likes that. Stela, over here. Stela, I'd like to introduce Bill, the Phoenix production director."
"Pleased to see you. We've already met ..."
"Yes. But we've never had the opportunity to work directly together."

Ronald interrupted. "Stela, Bill has a request to make." Stela turned towards Bill.

"Er! That is to say ... well, I've always been a faithful and loyal supporter of our chairman, and I think this acquisition is the best thing ..."

Ronald cut in. "Get straight to the point."

"Okay. As we know, senior management is being reorganized, and I'd like to apply for the post as head of US operations."

"That's a good idea, Bill," Stela retorted. "Everyone is free to apply for whatever they like."

"Yes, I know. But applying isn't enough. There's likely to be a lot of candidates. What I want is to win."

"So?"

"You're well placed, could you help me get the job?"

Stela frowned and turned to Ronald, with a dark look in her eyes. He was smiling. Stela spoke:

"Ronald, you won't hold this against me, will you?"

"No, not in the least."

"Could you hold my glass for a couple of seconds?"

"Yes, certainly."

Bill was dumbfounded and could not understand. Stela suddenly turned to him and pushed him with both hands into the swimming pool. Bill fell backwards, and hung in the air for what seemed like a very long moment before crashing into the water and splashing guests who were standing nearby.

Stela, with an innocent look on her face, turned to Ronald as she rubbed her hands.

"I think I did the right thing there," she said.

"You certainly did," replied Ronald, handing her the glass. Both of them burst out laughing.

"I've been hearing about him for several months now. What a relief to be rid of him. But, you're a sly devil, aren't you? You get me to do your dirty work!"

"That'll teach you not to make me feel ill at ease in public."

Bill got out of the water, helped by two German executives and the hotel staff. He was soaked through and looking sheepish. The crowd had come closer and was wondering why he had dived in. Bill said nothing. Water was streaming from his suit.

Gunther Plitsch, standing at the front of the crowd, asked Bill jokingly: "Is the water good?"

Bill saw red. He dashed at Gunther and pushed him into the water. After that, there was a general free-for-all in which Germans and Americans grabbed each other and threw each other into the swimming pool. Only two people escaped: Stela and Ronald, who had stood back from the crowd. They looked on in horror at this apparent degeneration of American–German friendship.

Passions had been inflamed by the alcohol. Once he was in the water, Gunther was the first to laugh out loud. Mike burst out laughing in his turn and then threw a large spray of water in Gunther's direction. This gave rise to a friendly water fight, causing great mirth. Stela and Ronald could not believe what they were seeing. They looked at each other and, without saying anything, jumped into the swimming pool to participate in this gigantic free-for-all. The noise brought the hotel staff running, but they did not dare intervene. After five minutes, some people started to get out of the water, holding on to each other. Germans and Americans helped each other out. Gunther climbed out of the swimming pool, with one arm around Mike's shoulders. He shouted in a booming voice:

"Mike, it's better for the merger to ship water today than tomorrow!"

Dripping with water, everyone burst out laughing. Mike kissed Gunther on both cheeks. The merger had been celebrated in fine style.

6.2. DON'T WORRY, WE KNOW WHAT WE'RE DOING ...

Stela, the Meletev human resources director, used the know-how accumulated from tens of acquisitions to manage the Brak takeover. Her story is a good illustration of the care taken in preparing an integration and dealing with those factors deemed critical for the success of the project. So, let's discuss the role played by experience in the success of an acquisition process.

Acquiring and capitalizing on experience

Experience has long been considered an important resource. This would tend to explain differences in performance between competitors in the same line of business. We can find proof of this in the work of the Boston Consulting Group (1971) on the experience curve. This curve results from a law that states, for a given product, there is a link between a decrease in its unit cost price and an increase in the quantities produced. This decrease in unit costs comes from three sources: economies of scale, experience and technological innovations. Economies of scale are linked to the quantities produced; technological innovation improves the process or the product technologies, which then leads to a radical change in manufacturing costs; the effect of experience is linked to time and repetition. This effect is explained by the ability of employees or teams to increase their productivity by improving their organization or their operating methods. From the accumulation of experiences come new ideas that are tried out and then put into practice.

In the case of strategic manoeuvres, especially acquisitions, there is undeniably the potential to learn. Very and Schweiger (2001) identified two distinct processes with which the acquirer is confronted: getting to know the target company and using past experiences. Since it is impossible to know everything in advance about the acquisition target, we have already pointed out that the buyer's knowledge progressively increases, as information is gathered, as surprises are encountered and as new things are uncovered. As time goes by knowledge of the target is enhanced. Every buyer experiences this target-learning process. Every acquirer takes part in this process, because his actions help to accelerate the learning process. For example, the acquirer can negotiate certain things he wishes to do in the target company: instigate a due diligence investigation as soon as possible or meet the target company's senior management. If the seller agrees, these actions will increase the rate of learning.

Very and Schweiger call the second process "the experience accumulation process". It concerns buyers who have already acquired companies in the past. The accumulation of experience consists in drawing lessons from manoeuvres that were initially undertaken to improve the management of a new acquisition. Contrary to the process of learning about the target, which is systematic, this second process depends on two factors: first of all, how much experience top managers have already had of acquisitions; then, their willingness to use knowledge to enhance performance. Frequent acquirers generally exploit the know-how they have picked up, as Meletev did with Brak. Let's have a closer look at these practices.

Capitalizing intelligently

Capitalizing on experiences in an intelligent manner consists in taking advantage of lessons learned in previous cases, then using these lessons to manage the new case more efficiently. The individuals involved in an acquisition operation are bound to learn from every difficulty, success or failure encountered. Nevertheless, it is important that this individual learning is turned into collective learning. In fact, the same people are rarely called upon for every acquisition, except certain experts like financial, legal or tax specialists. The latter are often assembled in a specialized unit like an "acquisitions department". Since every acquisition has its own particularities, it requires appropriate skills: here a specialist in this line of business, there a human resources manager, over there a production director and an environmental protection expert, ... Once the deal has been closed, the target company might be integrated into the acquirer's organizational structure or require a new senior management team. Consequently, the individuals and teams in charge of the integration are chosen in relation to the plans drawn up for the future running of the company: "The target operates in your sphere of activity: as you are responsible for this sector, you will be in charge of integrating the target". Or even: "The company we have acquired will be dismantled and each business will be merged with the corresponding profit centre in our company; human problems are bound to arise; that is why, as human resources director, you will be in charge of the integration." In brief, as every case is unique, a large number of employees are likely to be involved when the number of acquisitions multiplies. Individual learning therefore needs to be transformed into a collective heritage, so that the person who is taking part in the process today can use the knowledge acquired by his predecessors in the same role. Memorizing and exploiting the collective memory are the two components for capitalizing on experience.

To build this organizational learning, several means are used. These means depend on the nature of the knowledge: explicit or tacit (Nonaka, 1994). Explicit knowledge can be articulated in a precise manner then written down. Tacit knowledge is derived from action; it is difficult to articulate and is assimilated more or less consciously before it is used. In brief, the nature of this knowledge has an influence on the choice of means used for memorizing it and making it available throughout the organization.

Explicit knowledge is frequently codified. To manage the phase of hopes, some acquirers have created "acquisition manuals" that deal with several subjects. The first theme concerns the "right questions" to be asked during this phase of the process. The manual then contains checklists of areas to be investigated or points not to be forgotten (remuneration policy, contracts with the customers, patent rights, . . .). It may also outline key reasons for abandoning the process (e.g., when the target company's management has engaged in unlawful activities). In a recent survey into "deal-killers"[1] (Very and Schweiger, 2001), one person who answered, and who belonged to a large family firm, stated that negotiations should be called off if the seller demanded an exchange of shares in return for selling his company. Dossiers containing checklists and deal-killers deal with the transfer of declarative knowledge, describing concepts, categories or dimensions. The manuals sometimes deal with a second theme: how the team in charge of the dossier must interact with the company's decision-making bodies. For example, the manual indicates that the team must obtain the board's or the executive committee's agreement before starting any negotiations; or that the team must inform

---

[1] Remember: criteria that must be satisfied for negotiations to be pursued.

top managers if the price is no longer within the range initially established and ratified by senior management. They will have to get the go-ahead before pursuing discussions. This type of knowledge, which explains how to do things, is called procedural knowledge. To ensure coordination of actions within an organization this knowledge has to be transferred.

These are the two main themes contained in the documents relating to the study of an acquisition opportunity. There are apparently fewer documents relating to management of the phase of achievements. The explanation lies in the nature of the knowledge. A lot of the knowledge acquired during the phase of hopes can be written down as we are dealing with a fairly structured stage here. However, much tacit knowledge comes from lessons learned during the integration. Some acquirers do nevertheless share their experiences by writing up a textbook case. Employees likely to be involved in the integration study this case, which is an account of one of their group's past acquisitions. The case puts them in the situation of the team that was in charge of the integration. The participants analyse what to do and how to go about it. Then they have discussions with the people who actually worked on combining the companies. The case study them becomes a teaching aid at a training seminar on exchanging experiences.

To optimize the use of tacit knowledge, other companies have set up a system of "tutors". The tutor has already managed all or part of an acquisition process. During a new transaction, a person assigned to a task that carries heavy responsibilities can contact a tutor whose mission is to help him do his work effectively. With this object in mind, the buyer will have created a database containing details of past acquisitions: context and strategic objectives, how the operation unfolded, problems and solutions, as well as the names and roles of the people involved. From then on, anyone in charge of an integration process can consult the database and select past transactions that have similarities to his own case. After that, he can contact people who might be able to help. It is in the latter's interest to devote some time to passing on their knowledge, as there will usually be some form of incentive scheme that rewards cooperation. These types of systems also enable another sort of knowledge to be transferred: causal knowledge. The person receiving the knowledge can understand why such and such a problem arises and why such and such a solution might be useful with regard to the context.

It is difficult to pass on tacit knowledge simply through written documents. As the examples already described show, there has to be an exchange between people; this is the key to sharing and spreading this type of knowledge. This is what the acquirer has to encourage in order to improve the management of new acquisitions.

Information to be gathered, procedures to be followed, stories to be passed on or cases to be analysed: the codified aids that can help progress are numerous. The very fact of their existence leads to the conclusion that the role of people involved in an acquisition does not stop when their mission is successfully completed: this mission should systematically contain a review of lessons learned – sometimes called "project review" in project management techniques. This is the price at which the management of knowledge is likely to bear fruit. But does it really bear fruit?

Does experience in acquisitions pay off?

It would seem logical, at first sight, to associate experience with performance: the more knowledge the buyer has accumulated, the better his chances of success. The experience curve would therefore seem to apply to acquisitions. However, recent research appears to upset this relationship between the two variables.

Haleblian and Finkelstein (1999) found that the relationship between experience in acquisitions and the performance achieved in new acquisitions followed a U-shaped curve. The first acquisitions are fairly successful. Then the following ones are statistically less successful; eventually, the more experienced acquirer achieves high levels of performance again with his next acquisitions. In addition, new acquisitions that are similar to old ones are the most successful. Given the nature of the indicators used to measure performance here, one has to be cautious when using these results. Nevertheless, they are still disturbing. According to the authors of these analyses, inexperienced buyers tend to apply to any new acquisition the lessons learned during their first operations of this kind, irrespective of any resemblance between the new and the old acquisitions. Conversely, more experienced buyers, using the lessons of past successes and failures, first of all identify the similarities and the differences between new and old operations. They then select the lessons that will be useful and discard those that are not appropriate.

The link between experience of acquisitions and performance appears therefore to be more complicated than it should be. Hitt et al. (2001), in their excellent book on M&As, describe conditions and methods for learning, then formulate recommendations for actively managing learning processes. Nonetheless, they acknowledge that their guidelines do not guarantee success. More research is today needed to better understand the relationship between acquisition learning and performance.

In actual fact, there are many question marks around the comparison that was made with the experience curve at the start: as I have repeated since the beginning of this book, each acquisition is unique in its own way, unlike mass production that assumes there is a strong similarity between the goods being manufactured. Indeed, the heterogeneity of acquisitions may explain why the performance curve differs from the classic experience curve.

Consequently, the knowledge that is transferable to a new acquisition depends on the characteristics of this acquisition. This is why it is advisable to always keep a note of the context when accumulating knowledge, as in Table 4.1: managerial actions and decisions that bore fruit in a past situation may be worthless in another situation. That is why the choice of a tutor, whenever it is the preferred option, has to be based first of all on an analysis of the similarities between the projects. That is also why the codification of knowledge should systematically contain information concerning the context, so that an executive can determine whether this knowledge is relevant to the situation he is faced with today. According to Zack (1999), this is what much of the codified knowledge lacks: there is no reference to the context in which the knowledge was created and used. So, there is a risk that it will not be used effectively.

Other types of experience

Whether he is a seasoned skipper or a young cabin boy embarking on his first acquisition, the acquirer may be able to exploit other things he has learned, like his knowledge of the industry or the target company's country, or even his international experience, as illustrated in Figure 6.1.

Experience of the industry

There have been a number of studies on experience of the industry looking into the choice between expansion and diversification. The first research by Rumelt (1974) into diversification led to the following

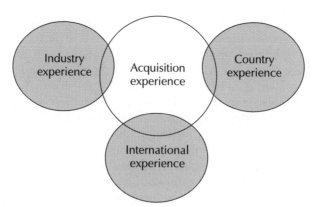

Figure 6.1 Types of usable experience.

conclusion: the shorter the distance – measured by the synergies – between the new activity and the company's current business, the greater the chances of success. This conclusion has not always been confirmed in later research studies. According to Bettis and Pralahad (1986), these mixed results are due to the confusion surrounding the definition of synergies. These authors suggest that there is some form of link between the two businesses: the dominant logic of management. A senior management team develops, with time and experience, mental schemes for identifying and analysing problems, and for implementing solutions that will help the company to succeed in its current business. The team has thus developed one or more dominant logics of management. When you are thinking of diversifying, the careless application of this logic to the new business could be inappropriate and might lead to failure. The context and the rules of the competitive game may be totally new and other ways of thinking become necessary. If there were no question of giving up the operation, it would then be better to recruit or acquire a company and retain its management. In this way the acquirers are likely to "learn about the new industry" and thus enrich their dominant logic of management.

Experience of the country

We pointed out in Chapter 5 how the institutional roots of a culture could create strong differences in behaviour that lead to misunderstandings between individuals and nationalities. For this reason, experience of the country counts: when asked about the difficulties they had encountered, many acquirers pointed to the marked difference between acquisitions in countries where they already operate and those in countries where they do not[2] (Very and Schweiger, 2001). According to this study, the whole acquisition process is affected by the level of knowledge you have of the target company's country. Figure 6.2 illustrates the case of an acquisition in a country that is totally unknown to the acquirer: every stage of the process seems to be affected.

  To remedy this lack of knowledge, buyers turn to complementary resources (e.g., consultants who are experts on local regulations and practices). Some buyers look in their own company for employees who are of the same nationality as the target company. If they find any, they include them in the team in charge of studying the acquisition. Their knowledge will help the team to decipher behaviour and to adapt forms of contact

---

[2] The difference does not appear to be as clear between their country of origin and the foreign countries in which they operate, although more research is necessary in order to confirm this conclusion.

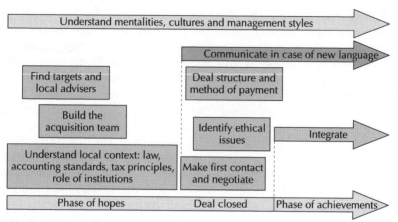

Figure 6.2   Difficulties raised when breaking into a new country.
Adapted from Very and Schweiger (2001).

and negotiating methods to the other party. In other words, it is not only acquisition specialists or the directors of the bidding company who have the experience that is likely to ensure the success of the operation. Other types of expertise, like knowledge of the country, can prove to be very useful for a successful outcome to the process. Moreover, when the acquirer already has operational units in the country, he often uses local resources to implement his project.

These efforts probably facilitate mutual comprehension between the different parties and help to close the initial gap that has been created by the scarcity of information. Nevertheless, research into the link between local experience and the success of an acquisition has come up with mixed results. It has not yet been proved that experience of a country has a positive influence on the eventual chances of success (Very and Schweiger, 2001).

International experience

Even if you do not know the targeted country, the fact that you have already acquired experience in the international arena can help. Frequent travellers develop the ability to listen and to analyse ways of acting and behaving. They have learned how to learn. They have learned how to understand. They have learned how to adapt. Consequently, they are supposed to acclimatize more easily when they arrive in a new country. That is why, if we follow this line of reasoning, it would seem opportune to involve such international experts in an acquisition project, particularly when the acquirer does not have any local resources. There have been very few studies on this subject, yet it deserves more attention in view of the fact that organizations are becoming increasingly interested in foreign acquisitions. This type of experience can be useful if it enhances our ability to deal with novelty or if it speeds up the rate of learning.

Vigilance and attention

In the end, this understanding of contextual differences or similarities, or having recourse to various types of experience bring us back to the concept of vigilance that we have already addressed in Chapter 5 dealing with the problems posed by differences between national cultures. As it happens, this notion of vigilance, which we associated with the experience of being involved in acquisitions, could easily have a negative impact on the link that exists between performance and other types of experience: industry, international, local, ... In brief, experience only bears fruit if the expert is vigilant when he is applying his knowledge. He needs to be on the look out, listening for the slightest signal: just like an actor coming on to the stage or the executive who is about to give a speech to a pack of journalists, the feeling of uncertainty is vital: it guarantees that his attention will be focused on his public's reactions.

The trailblazer of this concept Head (1923) who introduced it into neurological science. Head believed vigilance to be a physiological capability that makes adaptive activity possible. The levels of vigilance therefore translate the intensity in one's behaviour whatever direction is chosen (type of adaptation). Attention then corresponds to a level of vigilance called the phase of attentive awareness, and this refers to the ability to detect signals that are unforeseeable and faintly supraliminal (Buckner and McGrath, 1963).

Researchers in psychophysiology have studied the relationship between the level of vigilance (sleep, diffuse awareness, attentive awareness, emotion, overexcitement) and the level of performance achieved in a particular activity. According to Bloch's synthesis (1973), performance is weak in the phase of diffuse awareness and then tends to improve from the phase of attentive awareness right up to the point where emotions are aroused. Then, from a certain level of emotion right up to the point of overexcitement, performance tends to deteriorate, as behaviour patterns now become disturbed.[3] When learning something new, emotional activation (i.e., an increase in the level of vigilance) for a short period while

---

[3] This research helps to explain why phases of the process that are conducted in highly charged emotional atmosphere often lead to surprising results (e.g., the extra premiums paid out in relation to the "rational" price).

the knowledge is being acquired would appear necessary if this lesson is to be retained.

This little detour to look at other sciences therefore teaches us that memorization of a piece of knowledge seems to be the function of an optimal level of vigilance. In the case of an acquisition, an intelligent use of experience supposes that the expert is in a state of attentive awareness, ready to spot what is new or what is different in relation to his past experience. The company's senior management can help to maintain this psychophysiological state, by warning against overconfidence, by making people aware that each acquisition has its own characteristics and by preparing them to encounter a fairly uncertain world.

Carlos Ghosn, the director in charge of putting Nissan back on its feet after its acquisition by Renault, gave the following answer to a question about the choice of people (Emerson, 2001, p. 7):

"I think that the quality of an individual can always overcome any experience. Personal qualities are the most important element – the way you are and the way you handle things is much more important than experience. That said, I wouldn't say it's an absolute requirement for success to have multicultural experience, but it is a value-added. You really just feel more comfortable with someone who has a strong international or global background."

Summary

Does experience pay off? Certainly, but how? The link between experience and performance appears complicated. Experience of acquisitions seems to bear fruit when the acquirer is able to discern what knowledge will be useful and appropriate in the case of a new acquisition. For other types of experience, the link with success has not been confirmed. Nevertheless, the combination of experience with an appropriate level of vigilance (i.e., attentive awareness) could be the optimal combination for achieving a high degree of performance.

For those top managers who wish to build on their own experience, research findings suggest three things they should do simultaneously:

- Put in place a system of accumulation and transfer, based on the codification of explicit skills, on their availability, on coordination between people and on incentives to cooperate.
- Favour the sharing and confrontation of experiences by underlining differences and common points, by getting tacit knowledge to emerge from its context.
- Choose the people assigned to an acquisition project and prepare them to behave in a state of attentive awareness, on the lookout for

anything new. We all commit the sin one day or another of overconfidence. We need to avoid a consequent failure occurring in the case of a big acquisition, especially if there is an air of *déjà vu* about the target: indeed, we must remember the psychic distance paradox: the closer it is, the less attention we pay.

Finally, is there any greater danger than overconfidence, which can easily lead to falling asleep (and not noticing something new) or to arrogance (writing off something new as *déjà vu*)? We will leave it there for the moment, but we will come back to the subject of arrogance in Chapter 7.

Monitoring integration in time and space

7.1. STORY: SABOTAGE

Monday, 9:00 a.m.: A crime is reported

When I walked into the large glass building, I was immediately aware of the turmoil in the reception hall. A number of people, standing around in small groups, were talking and gesticulating; their words echoed on the marble walls and the hall resounded with this astonishing din. In addition, everywhere I looked I could see Dunpets, the toys manufactured by Dun. They were all over the place. The very latest collection, which would be in the shops in a few days' time, was exhibited along the walls. I was well acquainted with these toys that were all the rage with children: I had bought one of these horrible creatures as a birthday present for my son, and we now had at home a pet that talked, moved around and recorded our every action and gesture when we wanted it to – or, more precisely, when my son wanted it to.

My men were already here and they introduced me to the chief executive, Pierre Dunet. The big chief by nature of his job, but also by his size! Once the usual pleasantries had been exchanged, he launched into a vindictive speech about the damage caused to his company. Those who had committed the crime would have to be found and punished. It was not right to attack a company like Dun, which worked for the good of the community and provided a large number of jobs in the town ... The boss was not wrong, but his tone was unfriendly. He was taking his anger out on me. I expressed my sympathy and assured him that we would do everything possible to clear the matter up rapidly. He eventually calmed down and left me with his deputy, Loïc Renaut, a man who was about 45 years of age, sporty-looking and easy to talk to. He asked me to follow him.

I had been given very little information at the police station. That was why, as we walked down a long corridor, I asked Renaut to tell me what had happened.

"The first employees to arrive this morning noticed that their computers wouldn't work on the network. One of the IT people tried to identify the cause. He discovered that a number of cables had been severed, particularly the high-speed cables that link our head office to our other sites. It was sabotage, inspector. Whoever destroyed the cables knew that he would paralyse our system. He must have done it over the weekend. Here we are."

We had arrived in a computer room, or rather a back room filled with machines, and with a vast number of wires running everywhere, down from the ceilings, along the floor or between shelves. Even here, two Dunpets were lying on shelves. My men had cleared the room and had put yellow ribbon around the scene of the alleged crime to prevent anyone from gaining access. Only the IT technician who had discovered the damage was present. He showed me the hundreds of wires that had been cut. It could not have been an accident; that much was obvious. A person had done this. Probably someone who was not an IT specialist, otherwise he or she would have caused the damage in a much simpler way. According to the technician, it would take two weeks to repair the damage, reconnect and test the system. Dun would have to do without its IT system during that period. Fortunately, the data files had been automatically saved. The company's IT people were already working on a temporary solution, using the telephone network. Employees would be able to consult the files by the end of the day. So, work should resume rapidly in conditions that were almost normal.

One of my detectives recorded the witness's statement. Another detective asked who was authorized to enter this room. As the room had no windows, it was a fair bet that the saboteur had come in the front door, which required an entry code. There were no signs of forced entry on the door. I told my team to look for clues around the scene of the crime. A number of people had come to look at the room out of curiosity before we arrived, and this did not make our work any easier. Each member of my team got down to his task. As for me, I asked Renaut about any enemies the company might have.

"Frankly, inspector, I can't see who. Our competitors would never go this far. In any case, I don't think so."

"And internally, would there be someone with a grudge against you?"

Renaut scratched his head and thought for nearly a minute.

"It's true, there are tensions at the moment between various units within our group. But, there's a big difference between saying that and committing such a crime!"

I insisted that he tell me about these tensions. Dun had just acquired three companies: first of all, one of their direct competitors nine months ago, then, three months later, a holding company that controlled two of Dun's suppliers. According to Renaut, the acquisitions had stirred up trouble inside these companies, leading to strikes and confrontations.

I then asked him if employees who had been sacked or had resigned could be suspects. He did not know, but promised to contact the human resources director, who would give him an answer as soon as possible. I thanked him, told my men to meet at 2 : 00 p.m. in my office in order to make a first report then went back to the reception hall. People were now talking in whispers, and I felt dozens of eyes accompanying me as I left the building. And then suddenly I heard Pierre Dunet's voice booming out, followed by a stampede among the employees. The hall emptied. I opened my car door gently so as not to disturb the silence that now enveloped me. All the employees had gone back to work; it was as if nothing had happened at Dun's. Well, almost nothing . . .

Thursday, 10 : 00 a.m., at Svet's

"You have to understand, Svet has been taken over four times in seven years!" Jacques Dotten, the subsidiary's new boss, was explaining the attitude of the company's employees.

"When Dun took control of Svet, the staff said nothing. Usually you get reactions that are linked to a fear of losing your job or of a drop in salary. Here, nothing like that. The employees had already experienced three successive redundancy plans during the last eight years. Staff numbers have gone down from 300 to 100, so the 'survivors', as they call themselves, come to work just to earn their salaries. They don't put a lot into their work. As soon as I arrived, I realized this. A few days after my appointment, I gathered all the staff together and explained the reasons behind the acquisition and the role that Svet will occupy in Dun's strategic plan. There were no questions, no remarks and no protests. Then when we started to implement certain changes in our organization and management systems, we encountered passive resistance. The employees knew that Pierre Dunet had promised not to make anyone redundant during the first two years, but this decision did not make them feel any closer to their company. As long as the company exists, they will remain. They are very defeatist and expect nothing from the new management. And to think that there was talk of recreating a strong corporate culture! There's no longer any culture here! Commitment to the company has virtually disappeared.

I then said:

"Can we come back to what happened at the head office? Do you think that any of Svet's employees would have had reason to commit such a crime?"

Jacques Dotten thought for a moment.

"It's difficult to give a categorical answer. I personally don't believe that Svet people are involved. In fact, as they don't care about their own company, I can't imagine them holding a grudge against the new acquirer. Those who have survived four takeovers and then did not leave voluntarily certainly don't live for their work. They only come here to earn their living. They no longer react to what management imposes on them. As that is the case, why would they go and do something violent at the head office? However, I've only been in this job for six months, so I still don't know my employees very well."

I could see that he was still thinking as he talked. I let him continue his line of reasoning.

"If there is an avenue worth exploring here, it's perhaps research and development. In fact, Dun is exerting strong pressure on this department to speed up its rate of innovation. In Svet, we design and make the mechanism that enables Dunpets to move about. The overall concept for these intelligent toys is devised in Dun's, then sent to various partners like Svet who have to develop a subsystem that corresponds to the specifications. Here, we provide expertise in robotics: starting with a vague design and some specifications, we have to devise a Dunpet that is capable of moving in space and of reacting to its physical environment. So, the research department plays a key role. Svet's survival depends on their ability to think up solutions that can be mass-produced. We are now on the fourth generation of Dunpets, and it was Svet's fault that there were delays in bringing out the last two generations. That's why Dun's management is putting pressure on Svet's researchers, who have been identified as the source of the problem."

Dotten then suggested that I should meet the head of research at the beginning of the afternoon. According to him, this person was not very approachable. But he was an experienced manager and Dotten had every confidence in him. He organized the interview himself and then invited me to lunch. I declined the invitation: "never while on duty!"

So, at 2:00 p.m. in Svet's boardroom, I met the head of research and development. I had imagined him to be a long-haired researcher wearing a polo neck sweater. Instead I was confronted with a man wearing a dark grey three-piece suit, cufflinks and a gold watch. He also had a crew cut. Luc Reginald greeted me coldly.

"So you suspect us of destroying Dun's IT network ... That'll certainly help to improve my relations with Dun," he declared sarcastically.

"It's a very wide investigation, and we don't want to rule out a priori any leads," I replied. "Could you describe your department very simply and what the acquisition by Dun has changed for you."

"Of course. You're right, let's get off to a good start. My team is today composed of 12 members, specialists in electronics, automation and robotics. They've all been with the company for ten years or more. I'm sure you've been told that Svet hasn't taken anyone on for a long time. These past years, the company's attitude toward employees has been very dismissive, in every sense of the word ... Anyway, we work exclusively for Dun. They send us their toy project, with all its functions, and we deal with the 'mobility' part, that is to say everything concerning the movement of all or part of this robot: an arm that bends, an ear that waggles, an eye that winks, a toy that goes upstairs, etc. ... I have an excellent team. If we hadn't stuck together these last ten years, Svet would have gone out of existence. In fact, it's because we've always come up with original solutions to our customers' problems that Svet has been able to survive."

"Fine. Now I understand your line of work better. So, tell me what has happened since the acquisition by Dun."

Luc Reginald sighed.

"The usual mess ... The years pass by, so do the owners. Svet has been in financial difficulty for nearly a decade. Successive owners have made savage cuts in budgets and investments, without ever managing to improve our financial results. Today, not only do I have to work with a smaller team, a reduced budget and limited technical resources, but I also have to put up with my department being pounded by Dun's heavy artillery."

"What do you mean?"

"It's simple. Dun believes that the delays in innovation coming from Svet are linked to the way my team works and perhaps to a complementarity of skills between researchers. It's not so, believe you me. The delays are due to the reduced size of my department, in terms of human and financial resources. If they gave me an extra five million per year, my team would be able to create a prototype within the deadlines they imposed."

"So, your researchers are accused ..."

"If it was only that ... No, Dun has decided to audit our department. For two weeks now, we have been assailed by external auditors who have been told to identify our real skills, those that we lack and any problems with the way we work. They've even gone as far as studying the breakdown of my budget and our expenses. My people are fed up; some of them are on the verge of depression. If they could find another job of the same type in this town, a lot of them would already have left. Unfortunately, when you're tied to this area, you're stuck."

"Could these difficulties have incited any of your colleagues to harm Dun?"

"My people are so annoyed that they would be capable of many things. But frankly, inspector, I would be surprised if any of them was responsible for the sabotage. I've known them for a long time, they're all intelligent people and they know that doing something like that would change nothing. So, why risk your job for something illegal that will have no effect? If I were you, I would look elsewhere. You might find some leads worth exploring in SWA."

"I'm going there tomorrow," I replied. I brought this first interview to an end, thanked him and left. There was a really peculiar atmosphere in Svet. I took a big breath of fresh air out in the street.

Friday, 9:00 a.m., in SWA

I was greeted like royalty in SWA. The director's personal assistant gave me coffee and some petits fours and asked me to wait in a room equipped with a television and a games console. With one hand on the joystick I settled comfortably in the leather chair. When Bruno Cavi, SWA's chief executive came in, I struggled out of the chair and abandoned Lara Croft to her adventures. He was a very approachable person who made you feel at ease straight away. He decided to have a cup of coffee, asked me if I wanted another one and then we went into his office.

"Our company is very different from Svet. First of all, we don't do the same job: here, we specialize in audio signals. For example, when we work on the Dunpets, we deal with the toys' speech functions. You know that a Dunpet can record vocal messages that are directed at it, then reproduce them talking like a human being. Well, that is thanks to us. In fact, we have a very successful team of IT specialists and electronics engineers which is recognized throughout the world for its expertise in speech applications. That's why, unlike Svet, we aren't tied to Dun; we have a diversified portfolio of customers. And these customers have remained loyal over the years".

"If everything is fine, how did you end up part of the Dun group?"

"SWA is the original company in the holding that Dun acquired. The holding's shareholders were no longer able to invest in SWA, due to the problems they encountered after taking control of Svet two years ago. Svet was in difficulty; so, their priority was to invest in that company, but they never managed to refloat it. Meanwhile, SWA suffered from the lack of investment in its development. Our market is profitable, but you have to grow at the same speed as the market if you want to remain competitive. The shareholders couldn't keep up and they preferred to throw in the towel when Pierre Dunet made them an enticing proposition."

"Internally, how was the acquisition by Dun perceived?"

"The reaction couldn't have been better. The fact is that, unfortunately, SWA lost all of its management team in a plane crash two years ago, one month day for day after the holding acquired Svet. The two people who created SWA were like icons inside the company; the staff were very attached to them. Following this drama, the holding company appointed a new management team in SWA, but it didn't go down well. The employees had very little confidence in their managerial skills and accused them of not defending SWA's interests when resources were allocated to Svet. They also blamed them for the slowdown in growth and for the stagnation in profits that were already fairly weak. In reality, the employees were still attached to the company's creators, and the umbilical cord hadn't been cut. The new directors never succeeded in establishing their right to manage SWA. So, the announcement of our acquisition by Dun came at the right moment: most employees felt that it was now time to rediscover our dynamism and enthusiasm, after two fairly mediocre years."

"In brief, in your opinion, the staff is very happy ..."

"Absolutely, inspector. On the whole our people are satisfied with what they have found. That is thanks to Pierre Dunet's team who have been able to restore confidence. Pierre came in person to speak to us all. He explained the reasons for the acquisition and outlined his strategy. He confirmed that SWA would retain a lot of autonomy in managing its affairs and would continue to work for its usual customers. He then quoted figures for investments over the next three years and also pointed out that a certain amount of money was available now for the most urgent needs. He promised that people would be recruited for research and production. In brief, he convinced the employees that SWA was important to him. Two months after the acquisition, he also took a decision that dispelled for good any doubts or ambiguities. He brought SWA's remuneration and social security policies into line with Dun's, which were much better. The employees obviously appreciated this gesture. You should note that he didn't behave the same way with Svet."

"If you don't mind, can I ask you how you got the job of chief executive in SWA?"

"Good question. Beforehand I worked in Dun, supervising our suppliers. So, the SWA management knew me and we had good relations. That was why Pierre Dunet offered me the job. I accepted at once, as I was aware of the company's technological potential and I had received guarantees that I would be able to work with a large degree of autonomy."

"Let's go back to the reason I'm here: the sabotage in Dun. What you have just said leads me to believe that the perpetrator doesn't come from

SWA. What do you think? Despite the positive reaction to the acquisition, is there anyone here who might hold a grudge against Dun?"

"Hmm ... difficult question! Of course, I exaggerated a little bit when I said that everything was fine. To tell you the truth, there were a lot of exchanges in a short time between SWA and Dun. Pierre Dunet held open days at Dun for SWA's employees and he encouraged meetings between us. Everyone was then able to weigh up the pros and cons, could see the good and the bad sides of the acquisition and thus reached their own conclusions. I can't speak for every employee, but I know that a lot of them were very happy with Dun's dynamic style and entrepreneurial values. They also liked the team spirit and the clear definition of roles within the organization. Without being forced to, some of them have adopted working methods, planning tools and performance indicators used by their counterparts in Dun. On the other hand, they didn't like Dun's management control system. It was too cumbersome. They preferred our system, which was more flexible. Several SWA employees also noted a certain level of inefficiency due to the number of meetings that Dun's middle management had to attend. In SWA, there are not so many, and it's all the better like that. To sum up, an acquisition like this is never all black or all white. In the present case, it's light grey for most of the employees."

Bruno Cavi thought for a few seconds.

"As I'm new in this job, I can't judge each employee individually. I don't know them well enough. In any case, I haven't had wind of any complaints from any unhappy workers. As for the union representatives, they were in favour of the acquisition by Dun. At senior management level the old team has gone: I think they were quite happy with the terms they were offered in order to leave. I did have to restore some order into the middle management and reassign certain managers to new jobs. Some of them no doubt considered these changes to be a sanction, a loss of power within the organization. Logically, inspector, if they were to attack someone, it would be me, since I am the only one responsible for their so-called misfortune. Our new parent company is innocent: they were responsible for none of the decisions taken here."

We continued to discuss around this subject, but I learned no more. To get a change of air, Bruno Cavi offered to show me around the company. In this way I could get an idea of the atmosphere in the place. I gladly accepted.

Monday, 2: 00 p.m., in L3E

"Jules Dury, pleased to meet you." L3E's new chief executive greeted me 15 minutes late. "I can spare you 30 minutes, so, if we could get straight to the reason for your visit."

It was a fairly cool welcome and I felt uncomfortable. I asked Dury what his company did.

L3E was taken over nine months ago. It did not belong to the holding company that Dun had acquired. Unlike Svet and SWA who were Dun's partners in the design and manufacture of Dunpets, L3E was one of Dun's direct competitors. The company manufactured toys called Luckys, types of pets that vaguely resembled dogs. A child could speak to his Lucky, get it to repeat sentences and take it for a walk in the street. The mobility part of the toy was produced by Svet and the speech system by one of SWA's competitors. In L3E, they concentrated on the overall design of the toy and its video system. The Luckys' market share was increasing steadily, but had still not reached half of the Dunpets' market share in Europe. On the other hand, L3E had managed to break into the Asian market, where Dun had failed.

Jules Dury had been appointed as head of L3E one month ago, following the ousting of the former CEO, which had itself been decided on after many incidents that had occurred inside the company. First of all, there had been a fierce reaction from the employees when Dun had taken control. They had protested, inside the company to start with and then by alerting the media, against the threat of extinction which they faced. Dun has acquired our company in order to eliminate a competitor! Pierre Dunet had to intervene in person to try and reassure them. He had then decided to keep the old management team in their jobs, had guaranteed them a large degree of autonomy and had entrusted them with restoring confidence inside L3E. From Dun's point of view, retaining the old management team was a highly symbolic act, proof of their desire to ensure the survival of L3E. Unfortunately, under pressure from the unions who were still not reassured about the long-term security of jobs, the factory workers went on strike to obtain more guarantees as to their future. At the same time, Dun's salespeople complained about the behaviour of L3E's marketing and sales department, which was denigrating the Dunpets in order to persuade sales outlets to take Luckys instead. Not only were they denigrating the product, but they had also launched a price war that threatened to harm all of the industry's competitors. Order had to be restored quickly, so Jules Dury was appointed.

At the moment, things were quiet again inside the factory. Dun had had to make concessions concerning jobs in research and production. The strike was over. Nevertheless, the L3E salespeople were not willing to cooperate with their counterparts in Dun and the situation remained tense on the ground: competitors were now starting to take advantage of this internal quarrel to pick up market shares from the two companies. One of Dury's missions consisted in redirecting energies toward the market, while resolving the tensions between the two companies. An internal battle could only weaken the new group.

"You can understand, inspector," concluded Dury, "why I can only spare you a short time. Once I have finished this interview, I have a board meeting at which we are going to make a list of competent, motivated managers on whom we can rely to steer the company in the direction desired by Dun. We need at all costs to find champions of the deal, that is to say employees who support us and who will pass on reliable information in order to make a success of our combination with Dun. As the soft approach has failed, we're going to bring in a series of radical changes, for we have no more time to lose."

"Mr Dury, is there anyone in L3E who would have a good reason to sabotage Dun's IT system?"

"Hmm . . . Tricky question. A month ago, I would have said: everyone. Today, things have calmed down, and I can't think of anyone in particular. Apart of course from the ex-CEO who was ousted very abruptly. But I can't see a CEO cutting cables in an IT room. I've got to go, I've another meeting. Goodbye."

Tuesday, 10:00 a.m., back at Dun's

Few clues had emerged from our interrogations. The enquiries conducted by my people inside the company had produced no solid leads. As for my investigations in the companies that had been acquired, you could suspect everyone and no one. The answers to my questions lacked preciseness. So, I was expecting a lot from the team examining the crime scene. Unfortunately, here the results were also disappointing: there were a lot of fingerprints, and it was impossible to identify all those who had touched the cables. I decided to go back to Dun's to sample the atmosphere there and try to glean new information.

The head office was still in turmoil. This time, it was because of a meeting of the employees that had been called by their unions. They had invaded the entrance hall and were brandishing placards. One union representative, perched on a makeshift table, was haranguing the crowd through a megaphone. Loïc Renaut suddenly appeared out of the melee, shook my hand and took me to the IT room.

"Now it's our own employees who are demanding guarantees about jobs and working conditions! It's just what we needed, at the right moment too," he said, visibly exasperated.

"What sort of guarantees do they want?"

"The problem is linked to the acquisition of L3E. Our staff found out that measures were going to be taken to consolidate L3E and Dun, whereas we had initially planned to keep both companies autonomous. As both companies are in a similar line of business, the Dun people think that the merger will lead to redundancies. Since L3E is growing faster than

Dun in the field of intelligent toys, they are afraid that some of Dun's employees will be laid off: for example, in the international branch where L3E are more successful than we are. In addition, they have found out through their unions that salaries are generally higher in L3E and that their employees get one week's extra holiday. So, they are demanding that we align our salaries and working conditions with those in L3E. So, excuse me, I'll have to leave you for I have a crisis meeting to attend."

It was clear that life for Dun's managers was very turbulent at the moment.

The story stops here. At this point, it is possible to draw some pedagogical lessons from it. Nevertheless, the suspense endures. If you would like to find out who the guilty person is, read the rest of the story at *http://www.verymerging.com*

7.2. FROM THE INFINITELY LARGE TO THE INFINITESIMAL

"Sabotage" is the story of three acquisitions that differed in several ways (e.g., the acquired companies' financial situations or the strategic plan behind each acquisition). The problems are different, so Dun's teams have to manage each acquisition in a different manner. We have already looked at examples of difficulties in previous chapters; we have also talked about the role of the pilot and his teams. Now let's remind ourselves of what the phase of achievements is all about; that is to say, taking major decisions and selecting areas where action has to be taken. Some people will talk about global orientations, others will go into great detail about what action every unit, big or small, has to take: it's like going from one extreme to the other, from the infinitely large to the infinitesimal and, no matter what the level, questions of arbitration will arise.

Choosing the type of integration

Choosing the type of integration is fundamental. Employees are either anxious or hoping for opportunities in the face of expected changes, and they need a clear project in order to be able to picture the future being proposed to them. Visualization of the strategic ambition is necessary, but not enough on its own. It has to be accompanied by an outline of the road map that will lead to the final goal. By "road map" we mean everything that will be done in order to make progress in the required direction. Consequently, the integration communication plan, first of all globally then in a more detailed manner, is likely to provide the answers to many questions. Communication of this plan is also supposed to reassure interested parties outside the company: customers, suppliers and financial markets.

So, the integration proceeds from a global vision that has been adapted to the actual conditions of the merger. Haspeslagh and Jemison (1991) created an integration typology based on two factors, the need for strategic interdependence identified by the acquirer (type and size of the synergies to be exploited in order to create value) and the acquired company's need for organizational autonomy (in order to preserve its value). They singled out three types of integration:

- *Absorption* (strong need for interdependence and little need for acquired firm to have autonomy) leads in the end to a complete consolidation of the two companies.
- *Preservation* (little need for interdependence and strong need for autonomy) leads to the acquired firm retaining much freedom of action.
- *Symbiosis* (strong needs for interdependence and autonomy) often leads to a merger between equal partners, in which an entirely different company is created from the best resources and practices of the two organizations.

Figure 7.1 visualizes these three types of integration schematically. Haspeslagh and Jemison (1991) provided a very good description of these different approaches to combining companies. I would just simply add to this the fact that other variables come into play when choosing the type of integration: the relative sizes of the companies, the financial health of the target, the nature of the merger (hostile or friendly), ... These other elements need to be taken into account when deciding on the most relevant form of integration.

Each type of integration results in appropriate actions. For example, whereas preservation necessitates the installation of tangible barriers between the organizations, absorption results in the consolidation and standardization of a large number of practices. If it is a question of preservation, duplicate posts are retained as they are useful; they are abolished in the case of an absorption, often causing people to leave, which enables the company to reduce costs; duplicate posts are also eliminated in the case of a symbiosis, but the people are reallocated as far as possible to other jobs in the new organization. Implementation of the integration is therefore influenced by the type chosen.

One risk highlighted by researchers (Schweiger et al., 1993) concerns

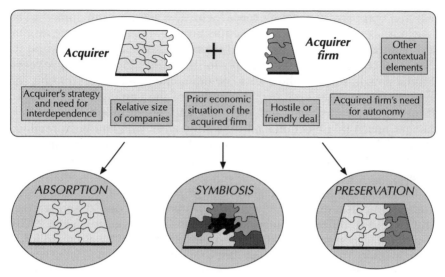

Figure 7.1 Choosing the type of integration.
From Haspeslagh and Jemison (1991).

how acquirers are attracted, consciously or unconsciously, to integration by absorption. The relationship between victor and vanquished, personal strategies, a feeling of relative loss or gain in status in the two companies, any of these might push the executives in power to want to mark the acquired company with their imprint. This in turn tends to lead to a desire to impose your vision of the world and your management practices on the other. So, the choice becomes absorption, just like some form of colonization. But, according to the typology mentioned above, a choice of absorption can only be justified when there is little need for the acquired company to retain its autonomy. Consequently, resisting the temptation to absorb is critical when there is a strong risk of destroying the acquired company's value. This is what Schweiger et al. (1993) state, and they suggest that a principle of minimum intervention in the implementation should be respected: any change that is not necessary should be avoided, particularly as behaving like a conqueror often leads to a display of arrogance that is plain for everyone to see.

Nevertheless, we should not go to the opposite extreme. The fear of being perceived as a colonizer or of imposing radical changes is misplaced. Vigilance should be combined with confidence. Prove your determinism, show your leadership, but avoid condescension and arrogance. When the situation is appropriate, go for an absorption. It is possible to impose large-scale transformations; indeed, the employees of the acquired company may even expect them. The acquirer can appear to be a saviour, as was the case in the acquisition of Millet in 1995 by Lafuma. Both companies produced and sold hiking equipment. Millet was on its knees and could not pay its creditors for the third time in as many years. Lafuma bought some of the assets, including the most important one, the brand name, and kept on a small number of the employees who had to adopt Lafuma's management methods and organization. The radical changes raised no objections, and the employees who had been retained considered themselves fortunate to be able to continue working for a brand that they cherished and inside a new group that guaranteed their survival.

Choosing the type of integration is an essential decision and sometimes a difficult one, especially when reflections on context and strategy tend to lead to different integration options (Schweiger and Very, 2003). Once the decision has been made, responsibility has to be assumed for it; consequently, the way the acquirer's employees behave is of prime importance. Their conduct must be exemplary and they need to be careful of its symbolic impact.

Handling changes in each organization's units

Par toutatis! Remember that most well-known of French comics, Asterix. It is the year 50 BC, and all of Gaul is occupied by the Romans ... All? No. One village of implacable Gauls still resists the invader. And life isn't easy for the Roman legions, garrisoned in the camps that surround the village ... The authors, Goscinny and Uderzo (1961), could have invented a cartoon strip about acquisitions. Indeed, their epic stories of Asterix are so similar to what happens in some acquisitions that it is difficult to tell them apart. Gaul has been turned into a Gallic–Roman world, but there is at least one pocket of resistance, and, as subsequent books about Asterix's adventures showed, other pockets exist in villages in Hispania, Corsica or Britannia and each one reacts in its own way. Julius Caesar's Romans adapt as they go along: they prefer to encircle the Gallic village rather than invade it.[1] So there is no homogeneity in the nature of the changes implemented at local level. And, there is no homogeneity in the way change is accepted by social groups locally.

Even if the type of integration chosen allows everyone to have a clear picture of the end result, it will still be perceived in different ways in various parts of the organization. The type chosen provides an overall vision of the integration philosophy, but leaves a number of questions unanswered in each person's mind. For example, absorption does not

---

[1] To tell the truth, in this precise case, they did not really have a choice!

mean that all the acquirer's practices will be imposed on the target company. On the contrary, certain ways of working in the acquired company are sometimes adopted by the acquirer. So, there is not one single type of absorption, but many forms. The action plan needs to be explained in detail so that employees can get a clearer picture of the transformations that await them. In addition, employees are concerned in various different ways by an acquisition depending on their company of origin, their job, their business unit, the country they live in, ... Where some people might be worried because they occupy a duplicate post, others might be more serene as they do not have a counterpart in the other organization. The extent to which they feel exposed to change and to danger varies from one individual to the other.

Whatever type of integration is chosen, the acquirer's reasoning is linked · to the organization's units (businesses, functions). Schweiger (2002) identified three main methods of change:

- *Consolidation*: physically combining the two organizations' units to create only one of each; for example, regrouping the resources allocated to two factories onto one production site only.
- *Standardization*: harmonizing working methods and practices without physically regrouping; the operations are kept separate, but are carried out in an identical manner; standardization concerns, for example, the transfer of best practices or the wholesale adoption of a competence initially possessed by only one of the companies.
- *Coordination*: coordinating the flows and the operations between two units; for example, selling one company's products through its new partner's distribution channels, or even manufacturing components that will be inserted into the other company's products.

The objective of all three options is to exploit synergies. Schweiger added a fourth possibility that is independent of synergies: *intervention*. This is action taken to improve the management of the acquired company and thus increase its intrinsic value. This option is applied when a poorly performing company is acquired. I would add in this category any actions undertaken to alter the organizational structure: in some cases of absorption, structural differences are abolished; once the units have been formatted in identical manner (on paper or in practice), it then becomes possible to consolidate or standardize. I would also include any actions aimed at socialization under the heading "intervention". Socialization consists in bringing individuals together in order to over-come problems of mutual comprehension or to initiate some form of acculturation. In the end, interventions have two objectives: value creation and the preservation of value through anticipation of or reaction to unexpected difficulties. A good illustration of this second objective is the case of an acquisition that combined two companies manufacturing custom-made telecommunication systems. During the integration, problems of a human nature arose: a group of engineers working for one of the acquired company's big customers suddenly resigned. The senior management had to reassure the customer the day after these resignations. A new team of engineers was sent as a matter of urgency to finish the work and to deliver the product to the customer on the agreed date. This type of intervention is an example of the desire to preserve the value of the acquired company, and, by extension, of the new group.

Each of these methods is to be found in Section 7.1's story, "Sabotage". Pierre Dun adapted a type of integration and the precise way he combined the companies to each one of his acquisitions. The story entitled "Fateful Encounters" also illustrates different choices for merging operational units.

An integration plan in principle should define these methods for every unit within the organization. An acquirer rarely standardizes everything; sometimes, he will coordinate some units, consolidate others, standardize methods elsewhere and let some of them continue to function as in the past. Of course, consolidation of units is more widespread when the acquirer opts for absorption. In this case, few units are spared by the transformations. This is also the case with symbiosis, when the two companies together design a new organization and new methods of working.

An integration plan is often prepared before the deal is even closed. Pressed by time, the acquirer cannot check the wisdom of his choices. From then on, it is up to the teams in charge of the integration to ensure as soon as possible the feasibility of the project. Are the profits expected from the synergies attainable? Wonderful from a distance, synergies sometimes prove to be less wonderful close up. The plan needs to be revised. Another factor can lead to revision: the price paid. A plan that is drawn up before negotiations have concluded may need to be altered when the acquirer pays more than the limit he had originally set himself. In this case, the management team seeks to get more out of the merger, which then encourages them to increase the scope of interventions and consolidations likely to bring in savings, even if they have to run the risk of confrontations or of losing key people. Ways to save costs are easier to find and exploit in the short term than ways to increase revenue.

Attention to detail therefore appears to be important. Differences in the policies implemented between units explain why the acquirer may encounter different sorts of difficulties in various parts of his organization. Here, consolidation meets with union resistance based on that country's legislation. There, people leave the company because working methods that they do not like have been imposed on them. Over there, customers are complaining about longer delivery times because the implementation of internal coordination has complicated product flow logistics. The infinitely large is linked to the infinitesimal. If the changes to all of his units, big or small, are prepared and applied meticulously, the acquirer can hope to make a success of his grand project. He is like a researcher in astrophysics: in order to understand the universe, he needs to define the elementary particles: photons, quarks, muons, ... The astrophysicist also relies on the work of experts in particle physics. In the same way, it is in the interests of the chief executive of a large group to delegate the detailed work to people who know their units very well.

However, perfection is rarely sought after in practice. Other imperatives influence the handling of the integration. The speed at which it is achieved is one of them.

A nice, quick job?

When executives are asked about the outcome of past acquisitions, they claim success, failure or even "success, but it took longer than expected". If Proust were still alive, he would note that many chief executives seem to be *"in search of lost time"*.

Since an acquisition is considered to be an investment, a deadline is set for creating the value hoped for. Projections of cash flows are worked out for this period. The implementation of changes is planned in relation to this deadline. However, as total anticipation of events is impossible, integration plans have to be amended as new things are uncovered post acquisition or when unexpected difficulties are encountered during the process. As shareholders and other interested parties expect results inside the time limits laid down, there is a great temptation to speed up changes in order to meet the deadline.

Strangely enough, researchers rarely delve into the subject of integration speed. In some contexts rapid integration, achieved in one or two years, appears to be the most suitable option. However, to the best of my knowledge, no study has ever corroborated this statement. When the employees of an acquired company are looking forward to change, it would seem logical to proceed swiftly. In certain countries, immediate transformations are demanded as proof of a new leadership: the United States, for example. This is what the French cement producer Lafarge experienced with its first acquisition across the Atlantic. After acquiring General Portland, the management team decided to spend some time studying how the company worked and was organized before implementing any changes. This approach was perceived as negative by the Americans who could not understand the purpose of an acquisition where nothing changed. How would value be created? This experience taught the acquirer a lesson and consequently Lafarge changed its approach. In a general way, it would seem that the objective of creating value for shareholders, one of the major goals of the last decade, is generating increasing pressure to integrate rapidly. Most companies listed on the stock exchange are subjected to this phenomenon. The reactions of competitors and customers are other factors leading to an acceleration of the process. When an acquisition involves big changes, the people concerned tend to devote most of their energy to resolving internal problems. Some competitors may seize this opportunity to attempt an aggressive breakthrough in their market. In the same way, customers who find that their relationship with the company has deteriorated are likely to look for a new supplier. Faced with an erosion of market position or the loss of some key accounts, it then becomes vital to react by speeding up the rate of change so as to concentrate minds again on the competitive arena.

Consequently, the quality of the integration can clash with the need to achieve profits rapidly. This dilemma was underlined in Chapter 5, which dealt with managing cultural differences. Quickly done does not always equate to well done. Let's have a closer look at this problem.

Designing appropriate arbitration processes

The essential role of the person in charge of the integration is in the end one of arbitration. With every unexpected event, with every difficulty encountered, a question of priority arises. As we have just seen, there could be a conflict between speed and quality. Speed is the rate of change imposed by the deadlines that have been set for achieving objectives. Quality is a balance between the needs expressed in the strategic plan, specifications and operational achievements. Costs must be added to these two factors. Every integration project has – or should have – a planned budget of costs associated with the implementation of changes. Resolving an unexpected problem may necessitate spending large sums on reorganization. Is it worth spending these extra sums of money? What will be the repercussions on the outcome of the integration, on quality or on the deadlines? In the end the decider acts like a referee and chooses between the three factors. Sometimes he will opt for one, sometimes for another.

For example, if he chooses in favour of quality, he runs the risk of lengthening the time taken to achieve objectives or of increasing costs. When the acquirer encounters problems in combining information systems, he can give his IT teams more time. The deadlines get longer and the cost of resources allocated – at a minimum the people – increases. It is also possible to favour two of the factors to the detriment of the third one. Whatever solution is chosen, it is highly likely that objectives will not be achieved in an area or areas that have not constituted priorities.

A team in charge of an integration in a transnational acquisition in the electronics industry were confronted with this type of choice. The type of integration chosen was absorption, and so the acquired company had to be carved up and inserted piece by piece into the buyer's structure. Several teams were set up to plan and orchestrate the integration: they worked either on a business sector that required consolidation, standardization and coordination, or on a function such as merging the salesforces, consolidating production units or extending the acquired technology (standardization), or even on consolidating systems and processes such as the information systems. The team supervising the project had to arbitrate on many occasions. For example, faced with problems in consolidating the information systems, it decided to postpone the deadline for installation, simultaneously increasing the reorganization costs. In this case, quality was the priority. The consolidation of the production units also encountered difficulties: here, the team decided to introduce the changes as quickly as possible, settling for a reasonable level rather than a perfect level of quality. Meeting the deadlines was also the priority when they extended one firm's technology throughout the whole group. In most arbitration cases, the decisive criterion was the speed of the integration when a problem concerned a transformation that was indispensable for creating extra value and achieving the strategic objectives.

In brief, as Figure 7.2 illustrates, the implementation of the strategic plan resembles a process punctuated by fairly frequent arbitrations according to the complexity of the operation and the occurrence of unexpected events.

The decisive criterion for choosing a priority remains the achievement of the strategic plan and the financial performance outlined in it. In spite of everything, however, it can still be a tricky decision in many cases. Changing course may prove to be a wise choice: here, in order to meet the deadlines, standardization replaces the planned consolidation; there, quality is the preference and the deciders plan interventions before carrying out the coordination that was desired. These types of local arbitrations, which concern a unit (function, line of business), are the responsibility of the teams in charge of the integration. Decisions taken locally are not necessarily insignificant: the choice of a priority could influence the evolution of the overall integration plan, if it creates a problem for the value creation project. Abandoning consolidation may thus mean having to do without the expected economies of scale. In such a case, the acquirer's senior management will have to arbitrate between staying on the course decided upon and diverting toward other

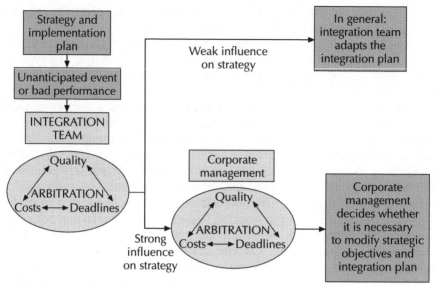

Figure 7.2   Integration as a sequence of arbitrations.

forms of action. If they stay on their course, it will mean accepting that part of the expected value will not be created; if they divert, they will have to find other ways to meet the objectives set at the beginning. This sequence of unforeseen events and arbitrations at several levels of the organization is what generates the strategic reorientations shown in Figure 4.1.

These types of arbitrations enable us to understand better why it is difficult to avoid a minimum of social upheaval during a merger. Let's suppose that the acquirer has started the merging process in a suitable manner and has rallied everyone behind his project. With the first difficulty that needs arbitration, each individual concerned by the decision will make his own analysis of the situation and opt, at least in his or her head, for a solution. However, their choices will not necessarily correspond to the decision made by the person in charge. From then on, the perception of the integration as a sequence of arbitrations helps to explain the emergence of tensions and opposition inside the new group. Attitudes and reactions will themselves generate new difficulties that will require decisions about how to handle the process. Tension and opposition may then increase or diminish as individual and collective perceptions evolve. In brief, events encountered and managerial decisions have an influence on people's behaviour as the integration progresses. This is why a well-designed monitoring system can help detect signals of problems or negative reactions and introduce mid-course corrections to the integration plan (Gates and Very, 2003).

Summary

Absorption, symbiosis or preservation; consolidation, standardization, coordination and intervention; quality, deadlines and costs; all these are the main components of the action plan that has been drawn up to obtain the results expected from the acquisition. The plan sets out the overall strategy and how it is to be implemented in each organization's units. The content of this plan will evolve and will also cause the project to evolve. Managing the content of the plan will require arbitrations that will favour, at a given point in time, one objective to the detriment of another. The work of the integration team may therefore prove to be complex if there are a lot of arbitrations. There will be a knock-on effect for the senior management, because most of the choices that tend to reorient the initial project need to be validated by those who hold executive positions. In other words, the acquisition process does not really stop when the contract is signed. The content of the integration plan will be subjected to numerous challenges. Paradoxically, the plan needs to be flexible in the face of fixed objectives. Most plans look to be straightforward when they are scrutinized during the phase of hopes. However, implementing the plan is like driving on a cold winter's morning. The road ahead looks straight, but patches of black ice, which are difficult to see or anticipate, cause the vehicle to zigzag on its way to the final destination. The story of the three acquisitions made by Pierre Dun is full of unexpected twists and turns, which call for adaptation and reaction. An integrator's life is certainly an intense one!

Conclusion

Acquisitions mesmerize executives, in view of the leap forward they and their companies can achieve. Acquisitions excite every manager who is curious and loves the unexpected. Acquisitions worry those who fear for their futures. Acquisitions interest those who are looking for the opportunity to advance their careers inside an organization. In brief, acquisitions rarely leave the people involved indifferent.

That is why handling an acquisition constitutes a test of management of the people by the people (or the opposite, as the famous French comedian, Coluche, would have said) in a specific context of change. Those who pilot the process are the key to the successful achievement of strategic ambitions; they have to manage other people's emotions, their relative loss of status and their moods. They also have to manage their own emotions and yet try to remain vigilant at the same time. They mark out the path, organize, arbitrate, monitor, communicate, rally and mobilize resources. They anticipate events and react. In synthesis, both the *quality of their management* and the *appropriateness of their behaviour* are likely to influence acquisition outcomes.

The stories and reflections set out in this book are examples of these types of action and behaviour. The book shows how far research and knowledge of the management of acquisitions operations have advanced. It also highlights possible avenues to be explored in the future, without knowing what lies at the end. Future investigations will no doubt shed more light on the acquisition process.

Throughout the pages of this book, I have presented this process from various perspectives:

- A process whose aim is to implement a strategic ambition that will have to be shared by the large majority of employees once the takeover comes into effect.
- A learning process, oriented in particular to accumulating and using experience appropriately.

- A process organized around a double project: acquisition, then integration.
- But, a process that needs continuity in its management, for there has to be a handover from the acquisition project to the integration project.

Each perspective has its lessons and enriches our knowledge, which remains, all things considered, fairly modest. If we want to advance further, we need to join together. Since we live in a time of free exchange, let's put the concept into practice.

Together we will write new stories based on your acquisitions. Thank you in advance.

Addendum

If you are reading this page, it is because you have a real desire to share your experiences. You were right to continue reading, because the conclusion on the previous page ... was not a conclusion! In fact, this book is only the starting point for a great adventure. From this point on, we should work together in order to advance further. With this in mind, please accept my invitation to join me on the Internet site dedicated to our future exchanges:

http://www.verymerging.com

The site has been designed as a complement to this book. It awaits you. It contains various headings under which you can share your knowledge with us, tell your own stories or ask questions. Nourish it as much as you can. The more there are of you who contribute to the site, the more we are likely to learn about how to handle acquisitions. These lessons and new reflections will then be reproduced, on the site or by other means. Why not a second book if there is significant progress?

So, I hope to hear from you soon via the keyboard!

References

NB: I have intentionally quoted few bibliographical sources in this book. If you would like more information about any particular theme to do with managing acquisitions, please contact me or use the website *www.verymerging.com*

You will also find many French references. A lot of good research has been undertaken in France (as in many other European countries), but this research is sometimes only published in the native language and therefore not available for non-French-speaking people. Hence, my reasoning for including references to articles and books written in French. Please contact me if you want more information about works written in French.

Aiello, R.J. and M. Watkins (2000). "The fine art of friendly acquisition." *Harvard Business Review*, **78**(6): 101–107.

Ashkenas, R.N. and S. Francis (2000). "Integration managers: Special leaders for special times." *Harvard Business Review*, **78**(6): 108–116.

Atamer, T. and R. Calori (1993). *Diagnostic et Décisions Stratégiques*. Paris: Dunod [in French].

Berger, P. and T. Luckmann (1967). *The Social Construction of Reality: A Treatise in the Sociology of Knowledge*. London: Penguin Press.

Berry, J. (1983). "Acculturation: A comparative analysis of alternative forms." In: R.J. Samuda and S.L. Woods (eds), *Perspectives in Immigrant and Minority Education*. Lanham, MD: University Press of America.

Bettis, R.A. and C.K. Pralahad (1986). "The dominant logic: A new linkage between diversity and performance." *Strategic Management Journal*, **7**: 485–501.

Bloch, V. (1973). "Les niveaux de vigilance et l'attention." In: P. Fraisse and J. Piaget (eds), *Traité de Psychologie Expérimentale, Tome 3: Physiologie du Comportement*. Paris, PUF [in French].

Boston Consulting Group (1971). *Perspectives on Experience*. Boston.

Buckner, D.N. and J.J. McGrath (1963). *Vigilance: A Symposium*. New York: McGraw-Hill.

Calori, R., T. Atamer and B. Dufour (1989). *L'Action Stratégique*. Paris: Editions d'Organisation [in French].

Castanias, R.P. and C.E. Helfat (1992). "Managerial and windfall rents in the market for corporate control." *Journal of Economic Behavior and Organization*, **18**: 153–184.

Charreaux, G. (1996). "Pour une véritable théorie de la latitude managériale et du gouvernement des entreprises." *Revue Française de Gestion*, **111**: 50–64 [in French].

Csiszar, E.N. and D.M. Schweiger (1994). "An integrative framework for creating value through acquisitions." In: H.E. Glass and B.N. Craven (eds), *Handbook of Business Strategy*. New York: Warren, Gohram & Lamont.

Dickie, R., A. Michel and I. Shaked (1987). "The winner's curse in the merger game." *Journal of General Management*, **12**(3): 32–51.

Emerson, V. (2001). "An interview with Carlos Ghosn, President of Nissan Motors, Ltd and industry leader of the year." *Journal of World Business*, **36**(1): 3–10.

Gallois, P.M. (1990). *Géopolitique – Les Voies de la Puissance*. Paris: Plon [in French].

Gates, S. and P. Very (2001). "Performance measurement during merger and acquisition integration." *EIASM Workshop on Performance Measurement and Management Control, Nice, France, October*.

Gates, S. and P. Very (2003). "Measuring performance during M&A integration." *Long Range Planning*, **36**(2): 167–185.

Ghoshal, S. and P. Haspeslagh (1990). "The acquisition and integration of Zanussi by Electrolux: A case study." *European Management Journal*, **8**(4): 414–433.

Giroux, N. (2000). "L'analyse narrative de la stratégie." *9th Conférence Internationale de Management Stratégique, Montpellier, France, May* [in French].

Goscinny, R. and A. Uderzo (1961). *Asterix le Gaulois*. Paris: Hachette [in French].

Haleblian, J. and S. Finkelstein (1999). "The influence of organizational acquisition experience on acquisition performance: A behavioral perspective." *Administrative Science Quarterly*, **44**(1): 29–56.

Hambrick, D.C. and A.A. Cannella (1993). "Relative standing: A framework for understanding departures of acquired executives." *Academy of Management Journal*, **36**(4): 733–762.

Haspeslagh, P. and D.B. Jemison (1991). *Managing Acquisitions: Creating Value through Corporate Renewal*. New York: Free Press.

Head, H. (1923). "The conception of nervous and mental energy; vigilance: A physiological state of the nervous system." *British Journal of Psychology*, **14**: 126.

Hirshleifer, D. (1993). "Managerial reputation and corporate investment decisions." *Financial Management*, **22**(2): 145–160.

Hitt, M.A., J.S. Harrison and R.D. Ireland (2001). *Mergers and Acquisitions: A Guide to Creating Value for Stakeholders*. New York: Oxford University Press.

Hofstede, G. (1980). *Culture's Consequences: International Differences in Work-related Values*. London: Sage Publications.

Jehn, K.A. (1997). "Affective and cognitive conflict in work groups: Increasing performance through value-based intragroup conflict." In: C.K.W De Dreu and E. Van de Vliert (eds), *Using Conflict in Organisations.* London: Sage Publications.

Jemison, D.B. and S.B. Sitkin (1987). "Acquisitions: The process can be a problem." *Harvard Business Review,* **60**(6): 107–116.

Larsson, R. and A. Risberg (1998). "Cultural awareness and national versus corporate barriers to acculturation." In: M. Cardel Gersten, A-M. Soderberg and J.E. Torp (eds), *Cultural Dimensions of International Mergers and Acquisitions.* Berlin: Walter De Gruyter.

Merali, Y. and P. McKiernan (1993). "The strategic positioning of information systems in post-acquisition management." *Journal of Strategic Information Systems,* **2**(2): 105–124.

Nahavandi, A. and A.R. Malekzadeh (1988). "Acculturation in mergers and acquisitions." *Academy of Management Review,* **13**(1): 79–90.

Nonaka, I. (1994). "A dynamic theory of knowledge creation." *Organization Science,* **5**: 14–37.

O'Grady, S. and H.W. Lane (1996). "The psychic distance paradox." *Journal of International Business Studies,* **27**(2): 309–333.

Pfeffer, J. (1980). *Power in Organizations.* Boston: Pitman.

Rebuffat, G. (1988). *Etoiles et Tempêtes.* Paris: Denoel [in French].

Rumelt, R.P. (1974). *Strategy, Structure and Economic Performance.* Cambridge, MA: Harvard University Press.

Schweiger, D.M. (2002). *M&A Integration: A Framework for Executives and Managers.* New York: McGraw-Hill Education.

Schweiger, D.M. and P. Very (2003). "Creating value through merger and acquisition integration." In: C. Cooper and A. Gregory (eds), *Advances in Mergers and Acquisitions, Volume 2.* Amsterdam: JAI Press.

Schweiger, D.M., E. N. Csiszar and N.K. Napier (1993). "Implementing international mergers and acquisitions." *Human Resource Planning,* **16**(1): 53–70.

Shleifer, A. and R.W. Vishny (1989). "Management entrenchment: The case of managers specific investments." *Journal of Financial Economics,* **25**: 123–139.

Very, P. (1999). "Ce que ne disent pas les chiffres." *L'Expansion Management Review,* **93**: 70–74 [in French].

Very, P. and D.M. Schweiger (2001). "The acquisition process as a learning process: Evidence from a study of critical problems and solutions in domestic and cross-border deals." *Journal of World Business,* **36**(1): 11–31.

Very, P., M. Lubatkin and R. Calori (1996). "A cross-national assessment of acculturative stress in recent European mergers." *International Studies of Management and Organization,* **26**(1): 59–88.

Whitley, R. (1992). *European Business Systems Firms and Markets in their National Contexts.* London: Sage Publications.

Zack, M.E. (1999). "Managing codified knowledge." *Sloan Management Review,* **40**(4), 45–58.

Index